Mary

Those Gold Plates!

Those Gold Plates!

MARK E. PETERSEN

BOOKCRAFT
Salt Lake City, Utah

Library of Congress Catalog Card Number: 79-63402
ISBN O-88494-364-X

First Printing, 1979

Lithographed in the United States of America
PUBLISHERS PRESS
Salt Lake City, Utah

THE BOOK OF MORMON
Is a sacred history of ancient America
Written about A.D. 400-420 by
Two divinely chosen prophets
MORMON AND HIS SON MORONI
Upon plates of gold bound together like a book.

"Wherefore, it is an abridgment of the record of the people of Nephi, and also of the Lamanites — Written to the Lamanites, who are a remnant of the house of Israel; and also to Jew and Gentile — Written by way of commandment, and also by the spirit of prophecy and of revelation — Written and sealed up, and hid up unto the Lord, that they might not be destroyed — To come forth by the gift and power of God unto the interpretation thereof — Sealed by the hand of Moroni, and hid up unto the Lord, to come forth in due time by way of the Gentile — The interpretation thereof by the gift of God.

"An abridgment taken from the Book of Ether also, which is a record of the people of Jared, who were scattered at the time the Lord confounded the language of the people, when they were building a tower to get to heaven — Which is to show unto the remnant of the House of Israel what great things the Lord hath done for their fathers: and that they may know the covenants of the Lord, that they are not cast off forever — And also to the convincing of the Jew and Gentile that Jesus is the Christ, the Eternal God, manifesting himself unto all nations — And now, if there are faults they are the mistakes of men; wherefore, condemn not the things of God, that ye may be found spotless at the judgment-seat of Christ." (Title page, Book of Mormon.)

TRANSLATED THROUGH THE POWER OF GOD
And Published by
JOSEPH SMITH, JR.
A modern American Prophet.

Contents

1

They Were Real

The gold plates given to the Prophet Joseph Smith for the translation of the Book of Mormon were genuine, real and authentic.

They were as real as the gold plates found recently in Korea. They were as real as the gold and silver plates found in the ruins of the palace of King Darius of ancient Persia.

They were as real as the gold, silver and magnesium carbonate plates of Sargon II of Assyria.

They were as real as the gold plates found at Pyrgi in Italy, and as genuine as any of the other Etruscan artifacts discovered in the area.

They were as real as the copper plates which were so carefully engraved and hidden away with the parchment manuscripts known as the Dead Sea Scrolls, and found among those scrolls in the caves of Qumran.

They were as real as the silver plates from India, which are beautifully engraved in the oriental language known as Pali and incised in Sinhalese script. These plates are relatively modern, believed to have been written in the eighteenth century. Copper plates, also written in the Pali language and incised in the Sinhalese script, have been found.

They were as real as the single sheet of gold engraved with modern Javanese manuscript, also believed to have been written in Central Java in the eighteenth century.

The gold plates of the Book of Mormon were just as real as those of Sargon, Darius, the Etruscans, the Essenes, or any others left by the ancients.

The engraved contents of these various metal plates were real, too. When Darius wrote about the boundaries of his kingdom as he engraved the plates later found in the ruins of his palace, he was speaking of established historical facts relating to his kingdom.

When Sargon spoke of his wars and vast construction projects, he was dealing in the literal history of his times.

And when Mormon and Moroni completed their abridgment of the ancient histories of America, covering a period from the time of the tower of Babel to within fifteen hundred years of the period in which we ourselves live, they, too, dealt with the realities of life — ancient life, vital, active, literal, physical life.

It was a life of intellectuality, and spirituality, too. It moved with love, but sometimes with anger; with faith and devotion, but sometimes in rebellion. It dealt with the human nature of millions of people who lived in America before A.D. 400.

Those ancients were not so different from people of today. They had their good times and their bad, periods of peace and of conflict, prosperity and poverty. It is all described there — engraved on the plates by Mormon and Moroni.

Although it may not be known to many who live today, the use of metal plates for permanent records was a fairly common thing in ancient times. Known from Java to Egypt, and from Spain to Iran, they date from millennia before Christ to as late as A.D. 800, and, in the case of the plates from India and Java, even as late as the eighteenth century A.D.

The manner in which they were deposited for safekeeping was similar also, even in these widely scattered sections of the earth. Nearly always they were found in heavy metal or stone boxes which in turn were hidden away, sometimes in the foundations of the palaces of the kings, in the ground, or, as in Korea, in an ancient pagoda.

Some plates were gold, some were silver. There also were copper and bronze plates, and even a few made of lead and tin, although the tin when found was usually badly oxidized.

Some plates had engravings upon them; others were plain. The translated engravings usually tell facts about their historical period. In the case of Sargon II, who governed Assyria in 720 B.C., a whole new vision of his reign and realm came into view as his records were read.

The discovery of the Darius plates gives authenticity to that monarch as a Bible character, for it was he who put Daniel in the lion's den, and later highly honored that prophet when he saw that the God of the Israelites protected Daniel from death.

The Etruscan plates found in Italy opened mysteries that have long prevailed concerning those ancient peoples, who lived, ruled and died in Italy from the eighth to the first century before Christ. They were the immediate predecessors of the Romans.

But not all of the ancient plates were found in distant lands. Some, although small, have been discovered in southern Mexico, twelve in one place, to be specific. They were of various sizes, the largest of which is five and a half inches long, compared to smaller ones which hardly differ in size from a postage stamp. Some contained writings in ancient tongues.

There are the Kinderhook plates, too, found in America, and now in possession of the Chicago Historical Society. Controversy has surrounded these plates and their engravings, but most experts agree they are of ancient vintage.

The discovery of many stone boxes has been a point of great interest. In Mexico and Central America as many as forty-nine such boxes have been found. Some were small and beautifully engraved, usually containing jewelry; others were large, probably used for food storage. But their existence establishes the fact that in ancient times stone boxes were commonly used, both in Mexico and in the Near East where the plates of both Sargon and Darius were found in such containers.

The gold plate story is a fascinating one, and is in no way limited to Joseph Smith and his plates. The extensive use of

Old World Writing on Metal Plates

Compiled by Franklin S. Harris, Jr.

Object and Material	Civilization, Place	Language and Script	Time	Remarks
Asia				
1. Gold plate	Javanese	Javanese	up to A.D. 1473	Now in British Museum, London.
2. Copper plate	Javanese	Kavi (old Javanese)	A.D. 1,300-1,500	
3. Gold sheets	Siam	Siamese		King's letters to princes.
4. Silver plates	India	Singhalese		2 x 18 in,; Buddha's first sermon; now in British Museum, London.
5. Copper plates	Harappa, Pakistan	Indus Valley script	3rd millennium B.C.	
6. Copper plate	Gorakpur District, India	Indo-Aryan	4th century B.C.	
7. Many copper plates	Pakistan and India		A.D. 324	Example: the Kesarbeda plates are three on a ring, text is a royal charter records of relics in a shrine.
8. Copper plate	Kalawan, Pakistan		A.D. 134	
9. Silver scroll	Taxila, Pakistan		A.D. 136	
10. Copper plate	Malabar Coast of India	Tamila characters	Middle 1st millennium A.D.	25 names in Arabic, Pahlavi and Hebrew characters.
11. Gold plate	India	Pali-Maunggun	5th century A.D.	Buddhist scripture.
12. Copper plates	India	Grantha script	5th-7th centuries A.D.	Inscriptions of Pallava kings.
13. Silver object	India	Mixed Pali-Pyu	6th-7th centuries A.D.	
14. Twenty gold leaves	India	Pyu characters	6th century A.D.	Pali scripture.
15. Gold plate	India	Pyu characters		
16. Bronze Buddha	India	Sanskrit in Gupta characters		
17. Gold and silver tablets	Persepolis, Iran	Trilingual: Old Persian, Elamite and Babylonian in cuneiform characters	518-515 B.C.	Darius I, 13 in. square, two pairs found at separate corners of palace.
18. Gold tablet	Hamadan, Iran	same text as 17		7.5 in. square.
19. Silver tablet	Hamadan, Iran	same text as 17		4.1 x 5.3 in.
Europe				
20. Plate	Portugal	Iberian		Found in 1876, mining regulations.
21. Lead, bronze, silver	Spain			
22. Plates	Roman	Latin	5th century B.C. to Roman times	Treaties between Rome and Carthage.
23. Lead tablet of Magliano	Etruscan, Italy	Etruscan	2nd century B.C.	Inscribed both sides; now in Florence, Italy.
24. Lead tablet of Volterra	Etruscan, Italy	Etruscan	6th century B.C.	Has about 80 words.
25. Gold plate of Tarquinia	Etruscan, Italy	Etruscan	3rd century B.C.	Nine lines of text.
26. Agnone bronze tablet	Italy	Oscan	3rd century B.C.	Long list of local divinities.
27. Bantia bronze tablet	Italy	Oscan	2nd century B.C.	Local laws.
28. Bronze tablet	Italy	Umbrian	Earlier than 500 B.C.	Acts of a corporation of priests, 19.5 x 11.3 in.
29. Base of a bronze pillar	Italy	Trilingual: Latin, Greek and Phoenician	160-150 B.C.	Found in Sardinia in 1860; now in Turin, Italy.
30. Bronze plate	Italy	Greek	4th century B.C.	Found at ancient Greek City of Thurii, Italy.
31. Bronze plates	Greece	Greek	5th century B.C.	Treaties between cities; now in Athens museum.

#	Object	Region	Language / Script	Date	Notes
32.	Bronze helmet	Greece	Greek	478 B.C.	Inscription presented to Jupiter Olympus by Hiero of Syracuse.

Egypt

#	Object	Region	Language / Script	Date	Notes
33.	Thin gold bar	Egyptian	Hieroglyphics	3000 B.C.	Inscription: "Menes" (the ruler).
34.	Gold plates	Egyptian	Hieroglyphics?	2800 B.C.	From tomb of Menkure, builder of the third pyramid.
35.	Gold leaf	Egyptian	Hieroglyphics	2000-1788 B.C.	Found at Lisht.
36.	Lead	Egypt	Pseudo-hieroglyphic		Found by Maurice Dunand.
37.	Silver tablet	Egypt	Egyptian	1254 B.C.	Treaty between Egypt and Hittites.
38.	Silver and gold tablets	Egypt	Egyptian	1198-1167 B.C.	Decree of Rameses III.
39.	Metal plates	Egypt	Demotic	After 4th century B.C.	Chronicle inscribed on 13 plates.
40.	Gold plate	Egypt	Greek	242-222 B.C.	Inscription for temple dedication.

Mesopotamia

#	Object	Region	Language / Script	Date	Notes
41.	Gold tablet	Sumerian (Iraq)	Cuneiform	3rd millennium B.C.	Found at Umma, modern Mesopotamia in 1937.
42.	Three copper tablets	Sumerian		2900-2425 B.C.	Temple inscription of ancient Adab.
43.	Copper	Sumerian	Hurrian language in cuneiform	2900-2425 B.C.	Found 1905, now in Metropolitan Museum, New York, and a similar one in the Louvre, Paris; temple dedication by Tisari, king of Urkis Urk.
44.	Bronze inscription figure	Assur (Iraq)		Mid 3rd millennium B.C.	
45.	Six bronze tablets	Byblos, Lebanon	Pseudo-hieroglyphic	2000-1800 B.C.	Found by Maurice Dunand in 1930s.
46.	Gold and silver plates	Assyrian		883-858 B.C.	Assurnasirpal II.
47.	Gold tablet	Assyrian		858-824 B.C.	Foundation record of Shalmaneser III found at source of Tigris, Iraq.
48.	Bronze plates	Assyrian			Found in 1876 at palace at Balawat; records campaigns of Shalmaneser III.
49.	Round silver plate	Assyrian	Hittite and cuneiform	9th century B.C.	Tarkondemos seal.
50.	Gold, silver, bronze, lead tablets	Assyrian		722-705 B.C.	Sargon II.
51.	Six bronze, one silver, one gold plates	Assyrian		722-705 B.C.	Found in foundations of Sargon II's palace in 1854.
52.	Lead plates	Mesopotamia	Mandean (of Aramaic type)	7th-8th century A.D.	
53.	Seven lead rolls	Assyrian	Hittite	7th century B.C.	
54.	Silver, lead plates	Semitic	Late Hittite	(600 B.C.?)	Found in 1950 in Beritz valley.

Palestine and Arabia, Turkey

#	Object	Region	Language / Script	Date	Notes
55.	Bronze tablet	Lower Galilee, Palestine	Ugarit cuneiform	14th century B.C.	Religious inscriptions; some now in British Museum, London.
56.	Copper or bronze plate	Palestine	Hebrew	12th century B.C.	Treaties of Romans with Jerusalem, letters from Spartans, Jewish events.
57.	Bronze tablets	South Arabia	Himyaritic	6th-7th century B.C.	
58.	Tablets of brass	Palestine		2nd century B.C.	Eight feet in length; religious writings.
59.	Copper scrolls	Dead Sea Caves, Palestine	Hebrew	Middle of 1st century A.D.	
60.	Gold and silver plates	Palestine	Hebrew-Aramaic	200 A.D.	Two sheets.
61.	Silver plates	Palestine	Aramaic script		Part of Koran; now in Evkaf Museum, Istanbul, Turkey.
62.	Copper plate	Maghreb (NW Africa & Spain)	Arabic		

such plates and their containers, whether stone or metal, provides abundant authenticity to the reality of such practices among the Book of Mormon peoples. They lived at the same time as most of the nations whose artifacts have been unearthed by accepted archaeologists.

In a hundred different locations, sixty-two in the Old World alone, have such discoveries been made. A compilation of most of these interesting discoveries was made by Dr. Franklin S. Harris, Jr., and published in the *Instructor* magazine in October, 1957. It is reproduced in the accompanying table.

Hugh Nibley, in *Since Cumorah*, mentions at least a hundred having been found.

2

The Brass Plates
of Laban

Highly important to the Book of Mormon are the brass plates of Laban, for they contained the same records as we have in the Old Testament up to the time of Jeremiah and Lehi.

They evidently were copied, probably on parchment or some other easily prepared material, and distributed widely among the later Nephites. Indeed, these were their scriptures, their sacred books, studied and believed by some, ridiculed and burned by others.

Quotations from the brass plates, particularly as seen in the defense made by Abinadi, and in the teachings of Jesus, are particularly interesting because of their close parallel to our own Old Testament.

Brass plates? Were they really of brass? Were they made of the same kind of metal which we know today?

The answer to that question cannot be given with certainty, but it is known that a copper alloy was called brass in Old Testament times. It is believed to have been an alloy of copper and tin, or some other base metal. In modern use, brass is what the dictionary calls a "yellow colored alloy of copper and zinc containing about one part in three of zinc."

Cruden's Bible concordance says this of brass: "Modern

brass, the alloy of copper and zinc, is not meant by the name in the Bible, as zinc was not then known. The word is generally used of a simple metal, and means copper. In other places it is properly bronze, the alloy of copper and tin." (Alexander Cruden, *Cruden's Complete Concordance to the Old and New Testaments* [Philadelphia: The John C. Winston Co., 1949], page 55.)

Peloubet's Bible Dictionary agrees with Cruden and indicates that the correct translation of *brass* in the Old Testament, would, in our terminology, be copper.

But the word *brass* appears frequently in the Old Testament, in fact as early as Genesis 4:22. Brass was used in their altars and in their courtyards. Goliath had a helmet of brass, and David "took much brass" from areas he conquered.

Rehoboam made shields of brass. Paul spoke of sounding brass and tinkling cymbals. (1 Corinthians 13.)

Is it to be wondered at that some of their sacred records were engraved on brass and kept in the custody of officials in Jerusalem?

Since it is well known that the ancients did engrave records on metal — even in the time of Lehi and Laban, for that is the period in which the Darius plates were made — would it be considered unusual for the Jews to do as did their neighbors?

In a dream the Lord showed Lehi that "Laban hath the record of the Jews and also a genealogy of thy forefathers, and they are engraven upon plates of brass." (1 Nephi 3:3.)

When the Lord showed Nephi, in vision, the coming forth of the Bible, he said: "It is a record like unto the engravings which are upon the plates of brass, save there are not so many; nevertheless, they contain the covenants of the Lord, which he hath made unto the house of Israel; wherefore, they are of great worth unto the Gentiles." (1 Nephi 13:23.)

Obviously, then, the brass plates of Laban were in greater detail than the Bible which was to go to the Gentiles, and which we now have.

When the people of Zarahemla were discovered, they felt highly pleased that "the Lord had sent the people of Mosiah with the plates of brass which contained the record of the Jews." (Omni 14.)

Mormon described in this way the destruction in America at the time of Christ's crucifixion:

"Behold, our father Jacob also testified concerning a remnant of the seed of Joseph. And behold, are we not a remnant of the seed of Joseph? And these things which testify of us, are they not written upon the plates of brass which our father Lehi brought out of Jerusalem?" (3 Nephi 10:17.)

They were indeed of great worth to the early inhabitants of America, and proved to be a blessing to them throughout their history.

Nephi wrote:

"And now when my father saw all these things, he was filled with the Spirit, and began to prophesy concerning his seed —

"That these plates of brass should go forth unto all nations, kindreds, tongues, and people who were of his seed.

"Wherefore, he said that these plates of brass should never perish; neither should they be dimmed any more by time." (1 Nephi 5:17-19.)

No doubt the writings of the Book of Mormon prophets themselves were made available to the Nephites, just as our modern scriptures are provided for us. But they also had, as their prior records, the Old Testament as it appeared on the plates of Laban.

Among the Israelites copper was used for many common purposes. Weapons, chains, temple lavers and other vessels were made of it. There were copper mirrors (Exodus 38:8) and copper helmets, spears, and breastplates.

Since brass was so commonly used and known by that name among the Israelites, even from the time of Genesis, it would be fully expected that their engravings on metal would be placed on brass, which apparently was plentiful.

Why not gold? Because they could mine copper in Palestine, but not much gold. They used the metal which was most available to them, and that was copper, together with its alloys. Apparently the Old World use of gold for such matters was largely reserved for royalty.

All of this becomes further evidence of the common utilization of metal for various purposes in ancient times, including the making and preserving of precious records.

3

Those Other Plates

The most publicized records on metal undoubtedly are the copper plates which were a part of the Dead Sea Scrolls. Like the other ancient records found at Qumran, they, too, were rolled up inside a large jar. They had been partially oxidized when found, and were very brittle. Because they were metal, and because of their oxidation, it was only with the greatest of difficulty that they were flattened out so that they could be read.

As with all of the scrolls, they, too, contained copies of Jewish sacred works, and now have been translated and published.

However, the interesting point here is that the records were engraved on metal. Those who scoff at the idea of ancient peoples making records on metal are left speechless in the face of this Qumran discovery.

Sacred writings on metal! Engravings made in Palestine! Records hidden away and preserved for twenty centuries! Found by accident, but recognized by scholars, they are now published to the world.

Is their credibility greater than that of the Book of Mormon plates? Both contain scripture. Both are ages old. Both came out of the ground — one from a cave, another from a hillside; one cased in a stone box, the other in an earthen jar.

Truly, the Qumran caves produced evidence of a practice that for many years was scoffed at by scholars who claimed that the only ancient records were those written on papyrus or cut into clay tablets with cuneiform characters. How times have changed! And how opinions must be revised as new evidence comes forth! The copper plates from the Qumran caves are new evidence, and that evidence is convincing.

But the other Qumran scrolls are also very interesting. One of them, containing almost the whole book of Isaiah, is a parchment scroll which, when unrolled, extends twenty-two feet. It was in a good state of preservation when found.

Another discovered a year or two later was longer still, measuring twenty-six feet when unrolled. It did not contain scripture, but was prepared for other purposes by the Essenes of that area a hundred years before Christ. It contained the statutes of the king, orders for the army, directions for temple building, rules concerning the observance of the Passover and other feasts, regulations with regard to cleanliness, information on the use of medicines, and comments on death.

The book of gold plates found in Korea is among the most interesting of the recent discoveries. It is known as the Keumgangkyeong-pan and consists of nineteen pages containing the Diamond Sutra of the Buddhist scripture engraved in Chinese calligraphy. These plates were discovered in December of 1965. They had been hidden in a five-story pagoda at Wanggun-ni, Cholla North Province, in South Korea.

The plates are 14.8 inches long and 13.7 inches wide. They are hinged together and can be folded up with one plate on top of the other.

When found, these plates were tied like a package by two golden cords and were enclosed in a bronze box. Other artifacts discovered with the plates date to the Unified Silla Dynasty of the eighth century A.D. This ancient golden record is now on display at the National Museum in Seoul.

The plates found in 1964 at Pyrgi, Italy, are also among the very interesting recent finds. They are seven and a half inches long and about half that wide, engraved in Phoenician letters, and were related to the dedication of a shrine for the goddess

Astarte. They provide evidence also that the Phoenicians were trading with the Etruscans of Italy by 500 B.C., before the rise of the Roman Empire.

The Etruscans, whose plates these are, were a powerful nation between 800 and 100 B.C. They lived in city states, which was customary in various lands in those days. There were fifteen such city states in that nation.

They were a maritime people, but mining was also a major industry. They strove with both Greeks and Phoenicians for the mastery of the Mediterranean Sea.

In 540 B.C., assisted by the Carthaginians, they defeated the Greeks in a decisive naval battle and then took over the coasts of Corsica.

Within a hundred years of this event the Etruscans began their decline. As their power diminished, that of the Greeks increased, both militarily and intellectually, a development which later influenced the entire known world, and in some respects still leaves its trace among us today.

As weakness developed among the Etruscans, the city of Rome also developed in strength, finally, of course, becoming the Roman Empire. The Etruscans were absorbed by their neighbors and lost their identity as a nation by about one hundred years before Christ.

An interesting people, they enjoyed great prosperity and erected many buildings, including temples, which resembled the Greek style of architecture. They built elaborate tombs for their dead, equipped with household goods, weapons and food to guarantee to the departed a safe and happy journey to the nether world.

Tradition and sculptured monuments reveal that the Etruscans enjoyed a luxurious and sophisticated life. Many of their customs were adopted by the Romans.

It is interesting that the Etruscans, like some of their neighbors, used metal for the preservation of their records.

Another find in the Etruscan ruins was that of three fragments of a tablet of lead twelve inches long. They were found in a pit or well near a temple built to Minerva, known as the goddess of wisdom. It was located at Punta della Vipera, near Cerveteri, Italy.

The tablet contains thirty-five completed words and parts

of fifty others, fragmented on the various pieces. Related to the rituals of the temple of Minerva, they are dated about 500 B.C.

The plates of Darius I, dated about 518-515 B.C., were found in the ruins of his palace at Persepolis in what was once ancient Persia. Today those plates are on exhibit in the Persian Museum of Antiquities in Teheran, Iran.

They were located in 1933 by members of the Iranian Expedition of the Oriental Institute of the University of Chicago, and translated by Professor Herzfeld. The workers unearthed two stone boxes, each containing gold and silver records. One box was broken, apparently from pressure of some kind, but the other was intact.

The records in the two boxes, identical, and engraved in three languages, said:

" 'Darius, the Great King, King of Kings, King of Countries, son of Hystapes the Archaemenian.

" 'Saith Darius the King, this is the country which I possess: from Scythia in Trans-Soghdiana to Kusha [Ethiopia], and from Sind to Sardis, which territories have been bestowed on me by Ormuzd, who is the greatest of the Gods. May Ormuzd take care of me and my kin.' " (Franklin S. Harris, "Gold Plates in Persia," *Improvement Era*, December 1940, page 715.)

Also found there were many stone tablets, one of which was in Elamite, two in old Persian and the others in the Babylonian language.

The gold and silver plates of Darius, seen at the Teheran museum, have been photographed many times, and a picture of them is presently published in the missionary edition of the Book of Mormon.

The plates of Sargon II are likewise interesting. They have been translated into both German and English. These valuable artifacts are known as the Votive Tablets of Sargon II. There were six such plates which date to the reign of this monarch in 722-705 B.C.

Discovered in a stone box, as were the Darius plates, they were made of various materials. Gold, silver, lead, copper, alabaster and tin were mentioned.

Two of the plates and their ancient container were lost in

the sinking of a ship on the Tigris River, May 23, 1855. The four surviving plates are of gold, silver, bronze and tin. The text was first published in 1867.

The archaeological report on these plates says that the use of gold for votive tablets (related to solemn vows) was not without precedent. There are four such tablets from earlier periods. One was related to the temple erected to the Assyrian deity Ishtar; another to the temple of Ishtar-Dinitu; another to the temple to Ishtar-Anunaitu; and the fourth to the Restoration of the sacred city of Assur by Shalmaneser II.

The plates declare that Sargon was great in both war and peace, and excelled over all his predecessors in the magnificence of his public buildings. He captured Samaria in Palestine and took full credit for it.

These votive tablets, which were found in the Khorsabad palace, are definitely dated at between 714 and 706 B.C. As the great king himself wrote upon them: "On tablets of gold, silver, bronze, lead, abar (magnesite) lapsis lazuli and alabaster, I wrote the inscription of my name and placed them in the foundation walls. Let some future prince restore its ruins, let him inscribe his memorial stele and set it up along side of mine. Then Assur will hear his prayers." (Daniel David Luchenbill, *Ancient Records of Assyria and Babylonia* [Chicago: University of Chicago Press, 1927], pages 58-59.)

A plate related to Shalmaneser III was found at the ancient city of Assur. It is in the Oriental Institute of the University of Chicago, where it has been since 1920. The translated text refers to the rebuilding of the ancient walls of Assur. A gold tablet that is only about the size of a postage stamp, it is covered with ancient writing.

If space permitted, similar stories could be written of each of the discoveries listed on the compilation made by Dr. Harris.

What a confirmation all of these plates are to the truth of the Book of Mormon and the manner in which its plates were preserved!

4

The Alabama Plates

The ancient Americans made written reports and endeavored to preserve them. Some were on metal, some on stone, and some on a form of paper which they had manufactured.

Although they have been examined by scholars, several of these ancient "finds" are regarded as being less than authentic, and hence are not accepted by archaeologists. Although still of wide interest, they have been a source of speculation and controversy.

One very interesting report that gives us little reason to doubt its authenticity is contained in a history of the state of Alabama written by Albert James Pickett (1810-1858), and published in two volumes in 1851.

Pickett reports that an Indian tribe known as the Tookabatchas came into the Alabama-Carolina area, and were absorbed by the Muscogees. Pickett then says:

"The Tookabatchas brought with them to the Tallapoosa some curious brass plates, the origin and objects of which have much puzzled the Americans of our day, who have seen them. Such information respecting them as has fallen into our possession, will be given. On the 27th July, 1759, at the Tookabatcha square, William Balsover, a British trader, made inquiries concerning their ancient relics, of an old Indian Chief, named Bracket, near a hundred years of age. There were two plates of brass and five of copper [about the thickness of a dollar]. The Indians esteemed them so much that they were preserved in a private place, known only to a few Chiefs, to whom they were annually entrusted. They were never brought to light but once in a year, and that was upon the occasion of the Green Corn Celebration, when, on the fourth day, they were introduced in what was termed the 'brass plate dance.' Then one of the high Prophets carried one before him, under his arm, ahead of the dancers — next to him the head warrior carried another, and then others followed with the remainder, bearing aloft, at the same time, white canes, with the feathers of a swan at the tops.

"Formerly, the Tookabatcha tribe had many more of these relics, of different sizes and shapes, with letters and inscriptions upon them, which were given to their ancestors by the Great Spirit, who instructed them that they were only to be handled by particular men, who must at the moment be engaged in fasting, and that no unclean woman must be suffered to come near them or the place where they were deposited. Bracket further related, that several of these plates were then buried under the Micco's cabin in Tookabatcha, and had lain there ever since the first settlement of the town; that formerly it was the custom to place one or more of them in the grave by the side of a deceased Chief of the pure Tookabatcha blood, and that no other Indians in the whole Creek nation had such sacred relics. Similar accounts of these plates were obtained from four other British traders, 'at the most eminent trading house of all English America.' The town of Tookabatcha became, in later times, the capital of the Creek nation; and many reliable citizens of Alabama have seen these mysterious pieces at the Green Corn Dances, upon which occasions they were used precisely as in the more ancient days. When the inhabitants of this town, in the autumn of 1836, took up the line of march for their present home in the Arkansas Territory, these plates were transported thence by six Indians, remarkable for their sobriety and moral character, at the head of whom was the Chief, Spoke-oak, Micco. Medicine, made expressly for their safe transportation, was carried along by these warriors. Each one had a plate strapped behind his back, enveloped nicely in buckskin. They carried nothing else, but marched on, one before the other, the whole distance to Arkansas, neither communicating nor conversing with a soul but themselves, although several thousands were emigrating in company; and walking, with a solemn religious air, one mile in advance of the others." (Albert James Pickett, *History of Alabama and Incidentally of Georgia and Mississippi* [Spartanburg, South Carolina: The Reprint Company Publishers, 1975], pages 81-83.)

One of the very interesting discoveries on stone, made in the United States, was that at Bat Creek, Tennessee.

Of this the Associated Press reported (as it appeared in the *Chicago Tribune* for Monday, October 19, 1970) the following:

"New York, October 18 — A Brandeis University professor said today evidence has been discovered that Jews fleeing Romans in the Middle East came west and discovered America 1,000 years before Columbus.

Wide World Photos

Stone found in burial mound in Bat Creek, Tennessee, in 1885.

"Cyrus H. Gordon, professor of Mediterranean studies at Brandeis, said the evidence is an inscription found in a burial mound in Tennessee in 1885.

"The inscription, he said, was found on a stone under one of the nine skeletons in the mound, but when the inscription was photographed and published by the Smithsonian Institution in 1894, it was printed upside down and its significance went unnoticed. The stone is at the Smithsonian museum in Washington.

"Last August, Gordon said, Dr. Joseph D. Mahan Jr., of the Columbus, Ga., Museum of Arts and Crafts, sent a photograph of the inscription to Gordon because Mahan was convinced there were connections between the Indians of the southeastern United States and the peoples of the eastern Mediterranean in ancient times.

"Upon studying the inscription, Gordon said, he discovered that its five letters are in the writing style of Canaan, the 'promised land' of the Israelites somewhere between the Jordan River and the Mediterranean.

"The fifth letter of the inscription, Gordon said, corresponds to the style of writing found on Hebrew coins of the Roman period. He translates the inscription to read 'for the land of Judah.'

" 'The archaeological circumstances of the discovery,' Gordon said, 'rule out any chance of fraud or forgery and the inscription attests to a migration of Jews . . . probably to escape the long hand of Rome after the disastrous Jewish defeats in A.D. 70 and 135.'

"Gordon, who presented the findings to a meeting of the North Shore Archaeological Society on Long Island, said scholars must now reassess other findings.

"In eastern Tennessee, for example, Gordon said, there is a group of people known as the Melungeons, who are neither Indian nor Negro, who are Caucasian but not Anglo-Saxon. They are, Gordon indicated, descendants of Mediterranean people and they believed that they came to the new world in ships about 2,000 years before Columbus.

"Gordon said the inscription was found in a burial mound at Bat Creek, Tennessee, in 1885 by Cyrus Thomas, who worked with the Smithsonian.

" 'Various pieces of evidence point in the direction of migrations from the Mediterranean in Roman times,' Gordon said. 'The cornerstone of the historic reconstruction is at present the Bat Creek inscription because it was found in an unimpeachable archaeological context under the direction of professional archaeologists working for the prestigious Smithsonian Institution.' "

THE PLATES OF DARIUS (Facsimile)

King Darius I of Persia, in commemoration of the
building of his great palace at Persepolis, placed two
metal tablets in a stone box in the foundation. The
engravings describe the boundaries of his kingdom in
three types of cuneiform: Persian, Babylonian, and
Elamite. They are judged to have been written about
518-515 B.C. (The originals are on display at Persian
Museum of Antiquities, Teheran, Iran.)

Close-up of Plates of Darius

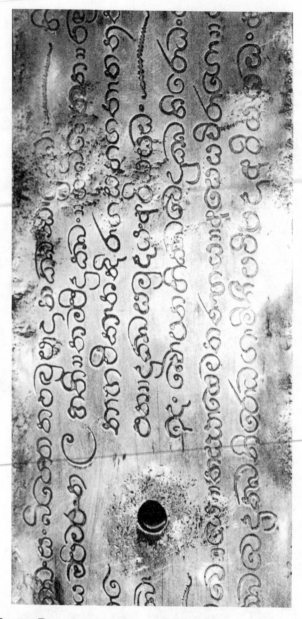

SILVER PLATES FROM INDIA (Facsimile)

This is one of the two plates that have been found that are believed to contain Buddha's first sermon. They are engraved in the original language known as Pali and are incised in the Singhalese script. (Originals in British Museum, London, England.)

PLATES OF SARGON (Facsimile)

The Assyrian palace of Khorsabad (built by Sargon II, 722-705 B.C.) was excavated in 1854. Discovered in its foundation were six small metal plates deposited in a chest. From a portion of the plates the words of King Sargon were translated: "On these tablets of gold, silver, bronze, lead ... I wrote the inscription of my name and placed them in its foundation walls." (Original in Louvre, Paris, France.)

BUDDHIST SCRIPTURE PLATES (Facsimile)

In 1965, nineteen gold plates were discovered in a
five-story pagoda at Wanggun-ni, Cholla North Province, South Korea. They contain Buddhist scripture
engraved in Chinese calligraphy. The plates had been
placed in a bronze box and deposited during the Unified Silla Dynasty of the eight century. (Originals in
National Museum in Seoul, Korea.)

Close-up of one of the Buddhist Scriptures Plates

KULKULCAN STONE BOX

Replica of box found inside the temple of Kulkulcan on the site of Chichen Itza, Yucatan, Mexico. (Original in museum at Chichen Itza.)

CARVED AZTEC BOX (Facsimile)

Many stone boxes have been found in Central and South America similar to the box described by Joseph Smith. Original of this box is in the Museum Fur Volkerkunde, Berlin, Germany.

HACKMAN STONE BOX (Facsimile)

Found in Texcoco, Mexico, and believed to have been made about A.D. 1500. The original was carved of basalt. (Original in Museum Fur Volkerkunde, Berlin, Germany.)

5

Early Uses
of Metal

New discoveries and more modern methods of determining ancient dates have changed accepted theories of some scientific researchers.

The Iron Age is no longer believed to have begun as late as 1200 B.C., and the bronze age did not necessarily begin even with 3000 B.C. Nor were all "Stone Age" men so completely engulfed in ignorance that they knew nothing of metals and could not have used them.

More recent research reveals that the processing of metals goes back as far as history and that the use of metal for the preservation of records was actually common among ancients — far beyond the time period usually ascribed to it.

For the Greeks, the Iron Age began about 1000 B.C. and for the Hittites as far back as 1400 B.C. These Hittites, who became one of Joshua's most feared enemies, are really credited with the origin of the Iron Age. They had their mines, some of which were even in the Balkans, and they exported finished metal to other lands.

Dating methods are passing through their own little process of evolution. Incredible as it may seem, tree rings are now being used to correct the errors of what was once considered to be the infallible carbon dating system.

The November 1977 issue of *National Geographic* magazine mentions such revisions (page 621) and adds that "some assumptions of the radio-carbon method have been shaken."

The magazine points to some specific instances in which dates are being pushed far back by the new discoveries. For example, it mentions that the Spanish tombs are now set back to at least 3100 B.C., far beyond the tombs of Crete "from which they were supposed to derive." It also points out that tombs found in Brittany "suddenly went back to an astonishing 4000 B.C."

And what is so interesting about this in connection with metal plates and ancient records? It is that some of these tombs yielded objects made of metal, some of them skillfully crafted, again indicating the antiquity of the use of metals.

National Geographic in this same issue points out that in Bulgaria, from graves dated as early as 3500 B.C., have come "rich finds of gold as well as of copper." They are considered to be "the earliest golden treasures so far found anywhere in the world." The magazine then adds that the find "carries our knowledge of goldsmiths' work back nearly another thousand years." It is interesting to note that the temples on Malta are now considered to be older than the pyramids of Egypt.

This certainly sheds new light on the intelligence of ancient men, and reveals that they were not all of the usually accepted cave man type by any means.

Ancients could read and write. They built beautiful cities, and some had inside plumbing and kitchens that no cave man architect could ever have devised.

Notable in all this is the fact that researchers are constantly changing their minds as new discoveries are made. It is obvious that no hypothesis based on incomplete studies can be regarded as the "last word." But the revealed word of God can be so accepted, for it comes to us through revelation.

Note what the Bible says about the early use of metals:

Tubal-cain, a figure from the book of Genesis, worked in both brass and iron. The experts say that the brass spoken of was most likely bronze, made of a mixture of copper and tin, since the zinc used in brass was not known in Old Testament times.

But in the time of Genesis iron was known and used, as well as copper and tin. It is likely that Tubal-cain lived about 3500 to 4000 B.C., far beyond the 1200 B.C. date usually given for the use of iron. (See Genesis 4:22.)

The land of Canaan was known for its "stones of iron." (Deuteronomy 8:9). And when did Job live? Who knows? Whenever it was, Job was acquainted with "iron taken from the dust." (See Job 28:2.)

From Moses' day onward, among the Israelites, it is recorded that iron ore was reduced in furnaces fired with charcoal and equipped with blowers. (See Deuteronomy 4:20; Ezekiel 22:20; Jeremiah 6:29.)

In the days of Moses, axes were made of iron. (See Deuteronomy 3:11; Numbers 35:16.) The scriptures speak of iron vessels, iron weapons and other implements of war, tools made of iron for farming purposes, iron engraving tools, iron gates, iron fetters, and even iron idols. (See Joshua 6:19, 1 Samuel 17:7; 2 Samuel 12:31; 1 Kings 6:7; Job 19:24; Psalms 105:18, and Daniel 5:4.)

Werner Keller, in his remarkable book *The Bible as History*, explains that the Egyptians knew about and used iron as far back as 3500 B.C.

An interesting thing about that, however, is that the iron they used came from meteors. They did no iron mining at that remote period.

It makes one wonder where Tubal-cain got his iron in the Genesis years. Did he mine it, or did he dig into the meteors that fell in his neighborhood?

But what does all this have to do with America and the gold plates?

As it is pointed out by the *National Geographic* magazine quoted above, metals were not all discovered in one place and then exported to other lands in ancient times. It is altogether likely, the article explains, that ores were found in various parts of the world at about the same time, quite independently in each case.

That was true not only of the Old World, but also of the

New, where gold, copper, iron, and tin were common. The Book of Mormon verifies that such metals had many uses, even in chariots for the armies, as well as swords, shields and other armor. But the early Americans not only used iron, as was done in the Old World, they developed steel as well. They also had alloys of copper and tin, and even used some hardening method for gold.

Although many of the archaeologists say that the ancient Americans had no iron, and used no steel, some scientific men now are looking at the matter in another light. For example, A. Hyatt Verrill in *America's Ancient Civilizations* writes:

"Can anyone actually believe, as archaeologists claim, that the colossal work [of leveling off a mountain at Monte Alban] was accomplished with crude stone implements and that the broken rock was transported in baskets carried on human heads? No one with an atom of common sense and a smattering of knowledge of engineering problems can actually believe that the Zapotecs cut away hundreds of thousands of tons of rock, filled yawning ravines and deep fissures with rubble, leveled an area hundreds of acres in extent and built huge, imposing structures all with no knowledge of steel tools, no explosives, no wheeled vehicles and no beasts of burden." (A. Hyatt Verrill and Ruth Verrill, *America's Ancient Civilizations* [New York: G. P. Putnam's Sons, 1953], pages 72-73.)

The Jaredites lived long before the Nephites came to American shores. They, too, had steel as we read:

"And they did work in all manner of ore, and they did make gold, and silver, and iron, and brass, and all manner of metals; and they did dig it out of the earth; wherefore, they did cast up mighty heaps of earth to get ore, of gold, and of silver, and of iron, and of copper. And they did work all manner of fine work.

"And they did make all manner of tools to till the earth, both to plow and to sow, to reap and to hoe, and also to thrash.

"And they did make all manner of tools with which they did work their beasts." (Ether 10:23, 25-26.)

In reference to this subject as it relates to the Nephites, we have this:

"And I, Nephi, did take the sword of Laban, and after the manner of it did make many swords, lest by any means the people who were now called Lamanites should come upon us and destroy us; for I knew their hatred towards me and my children and those who were called my people.

"And I did teach my people to build buildings, and to work in all manner of wood, and of iron, and of copper, and of brass, and of steel, and of gold, and of silver, and of precious ores, which were in great abundance." (2 Nephi 5:14-15.)

To say that the early Americans did not have these metals, that they were limited only to gold, and had only hand labor, with no metal tools is to ignore the facts in the case, as Hyatt Verrill points out.

So what do we have?

The ancients in both hemispheres did write on metal plates. They mined, smelted and finished metals on a wide scale.

They had skillful craftsmen who worked the metals.

Undeniable examples of their work may be seen now in public museums.

6

The Plates
of Mormon

The plates of Mormon were not shown to the world, but only to the Prophet Joseph Smith and eleven other witnesses.

But neither have most people in the world seen the plates of Darius, or of Sargon, or of Korea. Yet they take the word of those who have seen them.

Twelve men, including Joseph Smith, all of them American citizens of sound mind and unshakable integrity, saw the plates of Mormon. Those plates were handled, studied, and carefully examined by the witnesses, who signed solemn testimonies to this effect.

The fact that Mormon's plates are religion-oriented makes them suspect in the minds of many. But the Dead Sea Scrolls are religion-oriented, and so are the plates of Korea. So are the plates of Darius, who appealed to his god Ormuzd, and likewise the plates of Sargon, who built temples for the worship of his gods.

But Joseph Smith claimed that an angel of God brought the plates to him, complain the critics. Of course he did! But is that wrong? Did not angels appear to the apostle Paul? Did not an angel free Peter from prison? Did not an angel appear to Mary the mother of Christ and to Elisabeth the mother of John the

Baptist? Did not angels come to Abraham? Jacob wrestled with one!

Shall we cast away the Bible because it talks of angels? Is there not much that is supernatural about the Bible? Yet it is accepted, with all its angels and supernatural events.

Then why should we discard the Book of Mormon simply because an angel revealed its hiding place? The plates were real and physical and genuine. They were held and handled by competent mortal men. The engravings were carefully examined. The pages were turned over, one by one. Joseph's wife felt the record through a cloth covering. It was solid and physical and thus could be felt.

The witnesses were substantial men in their community. They did not lie. They had no occasion to do so. Would a local farmer or businessman who depended for his livelihood upon the good will of his neighbors deliberately lie to them and perpetrate a fraud upon them? Not likely, when it would be at the price of his earning a living. These witnesses were earnest and sincere. They did not deceive. They declared firmly that:

1. Joseph Smith, the translator, possessed and showed them the plates.

2. The plates had the appearance of gold.

3. As many of the pages as Joseph Smith had translated "we did handle with our hands."

4. "We also saw the engravings thereon."

5. It all had the appearance of ancient work and of curious workmanship.

6. "We have seen and hefted" the plates.

After all of this they signed their names to a document "to witness unto the world that which we have seen. And we lie not, God bearing witness of it."

This declaration was issued by eight men of integrity, all of whom were physical witnesses. They were:

Christian Whitmer

Jacob Whitmer

Peter Whitmer, Jun.

John Whitmer

These four apostatized from the Church, but never denied their testimonies. Also signing were:

Hiram Page

Joseph Smith, Sen.

Hyrum Smith

Samuel H. Smith

Of this second group, Hyrum Smith held so firmly to his testimony that he died a martyr to the cause. None of the entire group recanted. All maintained the truth of their declarations throughout their lives.

There were three others who not only witnessed the plates, but also saw the angel who came to Joseph Smith. And they heard the voice of God authenticating the entire proceeding. Of this they wrote:

"Be It Known unto all nations, kindreds, tongues, and people, unto whom this work shall come: That we, through the grace of God the Father, and our Lord Jesus Christ, have seen the plates which contain this record, which is a record of the people of Nephi, and also of the Lamanites, their brethren, and also of the people of Jared, who came from the tower of which hath been spoken. And we also know that they have been translated by the gift and power of God, for his voice hath declared it unto us; wherefore we know of a surety that the work is true. And we also testify that we have seen the engravings which are upon the plates; and they have been shown unto us by the power of God, and not of man. And we declare with words of soberness, that an angel of God came down from heaven, and he brought and laid before our eyes, that we beheld and saw the plates, and the engravings thereon; and we know that it is by the grace of God the Father, and our Lord Jesus Christ, that we beheld and bear record that these things are true. And it is marvelous in our eyes. Nevertheless, the voice of the Lord commanded us that we should bear record of it; wherefore, to be obedient unto the commandments of God, we bear testimony of these things. And we know that if we are faithful in Christ, we shall rid our garments of the blood of all men, and be found spotless before the judgment-seat of Christ, and shall dwell with him eternally in the heavens. And the honor be to the Father, and to the Son, and to the Holy Ghost, which is one God. Amen.

"Oliver Cowdery

David Whitmer

Martin Harris"

Peculiarly enough, these three men later rebelled. Angry with Joseph Smith, and fighting the Church, they lost their membership. Whitmer and his family set up a separate church of their own. But not one of the three denied his testimony published in the Book of Mormon! All remained true to what they said, even though personal conflicts took them out of the Church.

Oliver Cowdery and Martin Harris both returned to the Church. As they returned they bore testimony once again to the truthfulness of their original declarations. The plates were real. They saw the angel. They heard the voice of God. Joseph Smith was honest and truthful in his labors. The Church is true. So they solemnly reaffirmed.

President Joseph Fielding Smith told the following story of Oliver's return, as recorded in *Essentials in Church History:*

"For some time the Spirit of the Lord had been striving with Oliver Cowdery. Finally he decided to accept the admonition of the apostles given November 22, 1847, and again unite with the Church. He came to Kanesville with his family, in October, 1848, and asked to be received as a member in the Church. He had been absent for over ten years. A special conference was held October 21, 1848, at which Oliver Cowdery arose and confessed the error of his ways and gave his testimony as follows:

" 'Friends and Brethren: — My name is Cowdery, Oliver Cowdery. In the early history of this Church I stood identified with her, and one in her councils. True it is that the gifts and callings of God are without repentance; not because I was better than the rest of mankind was I called; but, to fulfil the purposes of God, he called me to a high and holy calling.

" 'I wrote with my own pen the entire Book of Mormon (save a few pages) as it fell from the lips of the Prophet Joseph Smith, as he translated it by the gift and power of God by the means of the Urim and Thummim, or, as it is called by that book, "holy interpreters." I beheld with my eyes, and handled with my hands, the gold plates from which it was transcribed. I also saw with my eyes and handled with my hands, the "holy interpreters." That book is true. Sidney Rigdon did not write it. Mr. Spaulding did not write it. I wrote it myself as it fell from the lips of the Prophet. It contains the everlasting Gospel, and came forth to the children of men in fulfilment of the revelation of John, where he says he saw an angel come with the everlasting Gospel to preach to every nation, kindred, tongue and people. It contains principles of salvation; and if you, my hearers, will walk by its light and obey its precepts, you will be saved with an everlasting salvation in the kingdom of God on high. Brother Hyde has just said that it is very important that we keep and walk in the true channel, in order to avoid the sand-bars. This is true. The channel is here. The Holy Priesthood is here.

" 'I was present with Joseph when an holy angel from God came down from heaven and conferred on us, or restored the lesser or Aaronic Priesthood, and said to us at the same time, that it should remain upon the earth while the earth stands.

" 'I was also present with Joseph when the higher or Melchizedek Priesthood was conferred by holy angels from on high. This Priesthood, as was then declared, is also to remain upon the earth until the last remnant of time. This Holy Priesthood, or authority, we then conferred upon many, and is just as good and valid as though God had done it in person.

" 'I laid my hands upon that man — Yes I laid my right hand upon his head (pointing to Brother Hyde), and I conferred upon him the Priesthood, and he holds that Priesthood now. He was also called through me, by prayer of faith, an apostle of the Lord Jesus Christ.'

"A few days later Oliver Cowdery appeared before the high council at Kanesville and requested that he be received into the Church. His case was considered and on motion of Elder Orson Hyde, who presided at Kanesville, he was received by baptism. When Oliver appeared before the high council on this occasion he said:

" 'Brethren, for a number of years I have been separated from you. I now desire to come back. I wish to come humbly and to be one in your midst. I seek no station. I only wish to be identified with you. I am out of the Church. I am not a member of the Church, but I wish to come in at the door. I know the door. I have not come here to seek precedence, I come humbly, and throw myself upon the decisions of this body, knowing, as I do, that its decisions are right, and should be obeyed.'

"It was a sad occasion, yet a time of rejoicing to see the former 'Second Elder' of the Church with a contrite spirit desiring fellowship in the Church, and the association of his former brethren. After his baptism he desired to go to the Salt Lake Valley and then take a mission to Great Britain. Before doing so he went to visit relatives in Missouri, and while there he was taken sick and died March 3, 1850. He died a happy man with the assurance that his sins had been forgiven him." (Joseph Fielding Smith, *Essentials in Church History* [Salt Lake City: Deseret Book Co., 1967], pages 386-87.)

Martin Harris journeyed to Utah, arriving in Salt Lake City on August 30, 1870. Of this President Smith wrote:

"He had been absent from the Church since the days of Kirtland; but had never during all those years denied his testimony. He now came back humbly to the Church, and was baptized by Elder Edward Stevenson and confirmed by Elder Orson Pratt. He died at Clarkston, Cache County, July 10, 1875, when nearly ninety-three years of age. A few hours before his death he discoursed on the Book of Mormon and reiterated the truth of the visit of the angel and bore testimony to the divine origin of the Book of Mormon." (Smith, *Essentials*, page 452.)

7

Lucy's Testimony

Lucy Mack Smith was the mother of the Prophet Joseph. She lived through the entire period of the restoration of the gospel and was intimately acquainted with each step, a personal, daily witness.

She was a truthful woman, deeply religious. She believed in God and she believed in her son. She knew Joseph to be an honest person. He never deceived her.

It was to his mother that Joseph first broke the news of his glorious vision in the Sacred Grove. It was to her that he came in times of persecution as a boy, when neighbors cruelly assailed him, and when one even attempted to shoot him. The bullet struck the family cow instead.

In Joseph's visitations with the angel, he was taught by Moroni concerning the plates, but also much about the ancient Americans themselves. He often discussed these matters with his mother and the whole family.

Regarding his first visit to the Hill Cumorah, Lucy Mack Smith wrote:

"When the family were altogether, Joseph made known to them all that he had communicated to his father in the field, and also of his finding the record, as well as what passed between him and the angel while he was at the place where the plates were deposited. . . .

"Joseph commenced telling us the great and glorious things which God had manifested to him; but, before proceeding, he charged us not to mention out of the family that which he was about to say to us, as the world was so wicked that when they came to a knowledge of these things they would try to take our lives; and that when we should obtain the plates, our names would be cast out as evil by all people. . . .

"I presume our family presented an aspect as singular as any that ever lived upon the face of the earth — all seated in a circle, father, mother, sons and daughters, and giving the most profound attention to a boy, eighteen years of age, who had never read the Bible through in his life." (Lucy Mack Smith, *History of Joseph Smith, by His Mother*, Preston Nibley, ed. [Salt Lake City: Bookcraft, 1958], pages 81-82.)

Following the first visit with Moroni on the hill, the family hoped that Joseph would be given the plates on his second annual visit to Cumorah. When he returned without them, they were all disappointed. Of this the mother wrote:

"He returned to the house, weeping for grief and disappointment. . . . As soon as he entered the house, my husband asked him if he had obtained the plates. The answer was, 'No, father, I could not get them.'

"His father then said, 'Did you see them?'

" 'Yes,' replied Joseph, 'I saw them, but could not take them.' . . .

"Joseph then related the circumstances in full, which gave us much uneasiness, as we were afraid that he might utterly fail of obtaining the Record. . . . We, therefore, doubled our diligence in prayer and supplication to God, in order that he might be more fully instructed in his duty, and be preserved from all the wiles and machinations of him 'who lieth in wait to deceive.' " (Smith, *History of Joseph Smith,* pages 84-85.)

It seems that when Joseph was in need of a scribe, it was his mother who arranged for Martin Harris to assist until someone else became available. She herself, of course, did not take part in the translation, but did all within her power to make conditions convenient for Joseph in his work.

When the translation was finally completed, a little meeting was held at the Whitmer home, attended only by those immediately concerned and members of the Smith family.

Of this she wrote:

"The evening was spent in reading the manuscript, and it would be superfluous for me to say . . . that we rejoiced exceedingly." (Smith, *History of Joseph Smith*, page 151.)

One night it appeared there was danger that the manuscript might be stolen. Of this she wrote:

"Oliver Cowdery came home that evening, and . . . said, 'Mother, what shall I do with the manuscript? Where shall I put it to keep it away from them?'

'Oliver,' said I, 'do not think the matter so serious after all, for there is a watch kept constantly about the house. . . .'

"I then placed it [the manuscript] in a chest, which was so high that when placed under the bed, the whole weight of the bedstead rested upon the lid. Having made this arrangement, we felt quite at rest, and that night, the family retired to rest at the usual hour, all save Peter Whitmer, who spent the night on guard. But as for myself, soon after I went to bed I fell into a train of reflections which occupied my mind, and which caused sleep to forsake my eyelids till the day dawned, for, when I meditated upon the days of toil, and nights of anxiety, through which we had all passed for years previous, in order to obtain the treasure that then lay beneath my head; when I thought upon the hours of fearful apprehensions which we had all suffered on the same account, and that the object was at last accomplished, I could truly say that my soul did magnify the Lord. . . ." (Smith, *History of Joseph Smith*, pages 159-60.)

It might well be asked if the mother of the Prophet, having gone through all these experiences, could have been deceived. She was a most practical and outspoken woman. She had deep perception. No deception could or would have escaped her. She knew the work was true.

The mother's intimacy with the outstanding events in early Church history is remarkable. She lived through it all, a personal witness. How anxious that mother was now for her son to succeed!

On the day designated for the three witnesses to see the

plates, the family assembled at the Whitmer home. The
mother describes how Joseph summoned them all to prayer
that morning. She wrote that at the close of their supplication,
Joseph turned to Martin Harris and said:

"Martin Harris, you have got to humble yourself before
God this day, that you may obtain a forgiveness of your sins.
If you do, it is the will of God that you should look upon the
plates, in company with Oliver Cowdery and David
Whitmer." (Smith, *History of Joseph Smith*, page 152.)

After the plates had been shown to the three young men,
again the mother was in a position to see the effects of that
manifestation. All three, with Joseph Smith, returned to the
house. Of this event the mother wrote:

"When they returned to the house it was between three
and four o'clock P.M. Mrs. Whitmer, Mr. Smith and myself,
were sitting in a bedroom at the time. On coming in, Joseph
threw himself down beside me, and exclaimed, 'Father,
mother, you do not know how happy I am: the Lord has now
caused the plates to be shown to three more besides myself.
They have seen an angel, who has testified to them, and they
will have to bear witness to the truth of what I have said, for
now they know for themselves, that I do not go about to
deceive the people, and I feel as if I was relieved of a burden
which was almost too heavy for me to bear, and it rejoices my
soul, that I am not any longer to be entirely alone in the
world.'

"Upon this, Martin Harris came in: he seemed almost
overcome with joy, and testified boldly to what he had both
seen and heard. And so did David and Oliver, adding that no
tongue could express the joy of their hearts, and the greatness
of the things which they had both seen and heard." (Smith,
History of Joseph Smith, pages 152-53.)

All of this makes Mother Smith an additional witness to
the truth of the Book of Mormon. She lived through these
events. She experienced them firsthand. It was no mythical
thing with her. It was real, actual and convincing. She knew
for sure, because she was there.

After the plates had been shown to the eight witnesses,
she wrote:

"That evening, we held a meeting, in which all the witnesses bore testimony to the facts, as stated above. [Here she refers to the signed statements of all eleven men, which she copied into her book.] All of our family, even to Don Carlos, who was but fourteen years of age, testified of the truth of the Latter-day Dispensation." (Smith, *History of Joseph Smith*, page 155.)

Here is the testimony of an entire family to the truthfulness of the work of Joseph Smith. It is so positive, so genuine, so impossible of refutation that it must be given most serious consideration by any and every thoughtful person seeking for the truth. That whole family could not create a fabrication. Neither could Joseph himself have produced an angel to testify to the witnesses; nor could he have falsified the voice from heaven declaring the truthfulness of the work. The family knew firsthand about these events, and the mother, in all seriousness and solemnity, recorded them.

One day a delegation from the local Presbyterian Church, to which she belonged, visited Lucy. Of this her account becomes another glorious testimony to the divine assignment which had been given to her son:

"Soon after they entered [the house], one of them began thus:

" 'Mrs. Smith, we hear that you have a gold Bible; we have come to see if you will be so kind as to show it to us?'

" 'No gentlemen,' said I, 'we have no gold bible, but we have a translation of some gold plates, which have been brought forth for the purpose of making known to the world the plainness of the gospel, and also to give a history of the people which formerly inhabited this continent.' I then proceeded to relate the substance of what is contained in the Book of Mormon, dwelling particularly upon the principles of religion therein contained. . . .

"After hearing me through, the gentleman said, 'Can we see the manuscript, then?'

" 'No, sir,' replied I, 'you cannot see it. I have told you what it contains, and that must suffice.'

"He made no reply to this, but said, 'Mrs. Smith, you and the most of your children have belonged to our church for some length of time, and we respect you very highly. You say a good deal about the Book of Mormon, which your son has found, and you believe much of what he tells you, yet we cannot bear the thoughts of losing you, and . . . I wish, that if you do believe those things, you would not say anything more upon the subject — I do wish you would not.' "

It was the deacon of the church who was the spokesman. Then Mother Smith, as she was called by her friends, turned to him and said:

" 'Deacon Beckwith, . . . if you should stick my flesh full of faggots, and even burn me at the stake, I would declare, as long as God should give me breath, that Joseph has got that Record, and that I know it to be true.' " (Smith, *History of Joseph Smith*, pages 160-61.)

Such was her testimony, although she never saw the plates themselves. How could any reasonable person reject such an affirmation of fact? Her affirmation stands with that of the witnesses. She would have died for the work. And she did give her life for it — every day for the rest of her mortal existence.

At another time, she bore her testimony that the Book of Mormon is true, that it was brought forth by the power of God and translated by that same power. She declared:

"I . . . say that the testimony which I have given is true, and will stand forever; and the same will be my testimony in the day of God Almighty, when I shall meet them, concerning whom I have testified, before angels, and the spirits of the just made perfect." (Smith, *History of Joseph Smith*, page 327.)

Following the martyrdom of her two sons, she passed through a period of tremendous sorrow and distress. But always she held to the testimony she had borne. Not even the death of her two great sons changed her conviction. Rather, it deepened her testimony, because now came revealed knowledge that they were divinely approved martyrs to the cause.

As she viewed the bodies of her sons, brought back from Carthage, she cried out in prayer: "My God, why hast thou forsaken this family!" And then came a heavenly voice in reply to her anguished question: "I have taken them to myself, that they might have rest." (Smith, *History of Joseph Smith*, page 324.) It was a revelation from God to a grieving mother. It was further testimony confirming the entire work. What a great witness to the truth she is!

During the conference of the Church held in Nauvoo on October 8, 1845, she was invited to speak to the congregation. Of this the official history of the Church records:

"Conference opened at the usual hour with singing and prayer.

"Mother Lucy Smith, the aged and honored parent of Joseph Smith, having expressed a wish to say a few words to the congregation, she was invited upon the stand. She spoke at considerable length and in an audible manner, so as to be heard by a large portion of the vast assembly.

"She commenced by saying that she was truly glad that the Lord had let her see so large a congregation. . . . She warned parents that they were accountable for their children's conduct; advised them to give them books and work to keep them from idleness; warned all to be full of love, goodness and kindness, and never to do in secret, what they would not do in the presence of millions. She wished to know of the congregation whether they considered her a mother in Israel, . . . [and] One universal 'yes' rang out. She remarked that it was just eighteen years since Joseph Smith the Prophet had become acquainted with the contents of the plates; and then in a concise manner related over the most prominent points in the early history of her family; their hardships, trials, privations, persecutions, sufferings, etc.; some parts of which melted those who heard her to tears. . . . She then mentioned a discourse once delivered by Joseph after his return from Washington, in which he said that he had done all that could be done on earth to obtain justice for their wrongs; but they were all, from the president to the judge, determined not to grant justice. But, said he, keep good courage, these cases are recorded in heaven, and I am going to lay them before the highest court in heaven. 'Little,' said she, 'did I then think he was so soon to leave us, to take up the case himself. And don't you think this case is now being tried? I feel as though God was vexing this nation a little, here and there, and I feel that the Lord will let Brother Brigham take the people away. Here, in this city, lay my dead; my husband and children; and if it so be the rest of my children go with you, (and would to God they may all go), they will not go without me; and if I go, I want my bones brought back in case I die away, and deposited with my husband and children.' " (B. H. Roberts, ed., *History of The Church of Jesus Christ of Latter-day Saints,* 7 vols. [Salt Lake City: Deseret Book Co., 1970], vol. 7, pages 470-71; hereafter cited as *DHC.*)

Her children, however, chose to remain in Illinois, since some of them were in conflict with Brigham Young. She remained with them, being too old and weak to undertake the long overland journey to the Great Basin. She died about ten years after making this farewell address, loyal to the Church and to its leader, Brigham Young, but unable, because of circumstances, to join the Saints in the West.

When Enoch B. Tripp spoke in the Salt Lake Tabernacle on September 7, 1856, he reported a personal visit to Mother Lucy Smith, quoting her own words in this manner:

" 'Enoch, I am glad to again see you; I am glad to see a man again from Salt Lake.' She cried for joy, and said she had desired for two years to be with the saints in the valleys of the mountains. She also said, 'Give my love to Brigham and Heber and all the faithful saints, for my heart is with them.' " (Journal History of The Church of Jesus Christ of Latter-day Saints, September 7, 1856, page 4.)

Such was the testimony of Mother Lucy Mack Smith. She knew full well the story of the gold plates, and of the events which followed their transmittal to her son Joseph by the angel Moroni. She gave all the years of her life for the cause. She knew by personal experience that it was all true!

8

Translating
the Plates

The Book of Mormon plates were engraved in a language unknown to modern men. The Nephites called it Reformed Egyptian. Of this Moroni wrote:

"And now, behold, we have written this record according to our knowledge, in the characters which are called among us the reformed Egyptian, being handed down and altered by us, according to our manner of speech.

"And if our plates had been sufficiently large we should have written in Hebrew; but the Hebrew hath been altered by us also; and if we could have written in Hebrew, behold, ye would have had no imperfection in our record.

"But the Lord knoweth the things which we have written, and also that none other people knoweth our language; therefore he hath prepared means for the interpretation thereof." (Mormon 9:32-34.)

How could Joseph Smith translate such an unknown language unless he was given divine aid? He was poorly educated. When Isaiah predicted the coming forth of the book (Isaiah 29:12), he said it would be given to an unlearned man, and such indeed was Joseph Smith when but a youth.

Dr. John A. Widtsoe wrote the following in his book on the life of the Prophet Joseph:

"Joseph Smith's mother wrote that of all her children he was the least inclined to give his time to the reading of books. He was fond of outdoor life, and physical games. His history mentions wrestling matches, jumping, and ball playing. Children grown to manhood related the story of games with the Prophet.

"He grew up used to hard work. His father was chiefly a farmer in the Palmyra days. Joseph had to take his share in the labors on the farm. When their farm labors permitted he sought employment elsewhere.... He writes in his journal that he was obliged to earn a scant living by the toil of his hands.

"His school education was very meager. He could read, write an imperfect hand, and knew enough arithmetic for his needs. In the words of Orson Pratt who lived in his house, and became his great defender:

" 'His advantages for acquiring scientific knowledge were exceedingly small, being limited to a slight acquaintance with two or three of the common branches of learning. He could read without much difficulty, and write a very imperfect hand; and had a very limited understanding of the elementary rules of arithmetic. These were his highest and only attainments; while the rest of those branches, so universally taught in the common schools throughout the United States, were entirely unknown to him.'

"However, he had a fine mind. All who knew him, friend and foe, conceded that his mental ability was high....

"In short, Joseph Smith was not better educated than the average boy of his pioneer period, from a family reduced to poverty, inured to toil with little chance for an education." (John A. Widtsoe, *Joseph Smith: Seeker After Truth, Prophet of God* [Salt Lake City: Bookcraft, 1957], pages 67-68.)

Of course, in his later years Joseph Smith became a brilliant student of various languages, of some of the sciences of the day, and certainly of religion, for Divinity taught him by revelation and by angelic ministry.

But in his youth, when the Book of Mormon plates were

given to him, he was an unlearned man, with hardly more than what we of today would call a sixth-grade education.

Yet the Book of Mormon is a religious and a literary masterpiece. It is a miracle, wrought by the power of God through the instrumentality of an unlearned youth. It is far beyond the fondest dreams or abilities of any farm boy. It is revelation!

Let us consider the actual translation of this record. Joseph Smith says he did it by the gift and power of God, through the use of the Urim and Thummim. As unlearned as he was at that time in his life, he could have done it in no other way.

Enemies arose. They sought to destroy not only the Prophet Joseph himself, but also his work. They endeavored at every point to discredit what he did, to vilify and tarnish his innocent name, and to downgrade his labors. They would not admit that he was a prophet. They did not believe in modern revelation. They sought only to debase him and abuse and defame him.

So it was that they tried to obliterate the divine stamp on his translation of the Book of Mormon. They determined to "humanize" his work by saying that he himself had composed the volume, or that he stole it from Spaulding, or that Sidney Rigdon wrote it, although it was published well before Joseph ever heard of Sidney Rigdon.

In their effort to "humanize" his work of translation, they grudgingly gave him credit for knowledge and skills which he did not have, saying that he plagiarized parts of the Bible and that he literally took whole chapters out of it to compose his Book of Mormon — claims which, of course, were untrue and ridiculous.

Joseph Smith declared that he wrote only under the gift and power of God. Oliver Cowdery, his scribe, said the same thing, adding, "I wrote with my own pen the entire Book of Mormon (save a few pages) as it fell from the lips of the Prophet (Joseph Smith) as he translated it by the gift and power of God." (Journal of Reuben Miller, October 21, 1848.)

Martin Harris, another assistant scribe, bore the same testimony. And Emma Smith, the beloved wife of the Prophet, who literally lived in and with and through this translation period, and assisted at times as a scribe, bore this testimony:

"I am satisfied that no man could have dictated the writing of the manuscripts unless he was inspired; for, when acting as his scribe, . . . [Joseph] would dictate to me hour after hour; and when returning after meals, or after interruptions, he would at once begin where he had left off, without either seeing the manuscript or having any portion of it read to him. . . . It would have been improbable that a learned man could do this; and for one so . . . unlearned as he was, it was simply impossible." (*The Saints' Herald,* 1879, 26:290.)

Then how can critics truthfully say that Joseph Smith, in his youth, was so scholarly that he could or would deliberately take passages from the Bible and skillfully make it appear that they were part of the Book of Mormon manuscript?

His mother said that at that early point in his life he had not yet even read through the Bible. Then how could he select carefully chosen passages and work them into the Book of Mormon text appropriately and skillfully?

Not having read through the Bible in his early years, he had no adequate knowledge with which to do such an editing job even if he had been adept at writing or editing, neither of which skills he possessed that early in life.

Read, for example, some of the Savior's beautiful sermons in the Book of Mormon. Note that the Lord quotes Bible prophets. Are we to say that the unlearned Joseph Smith had the audacity or the skill to rewrite the Savior's sermons and insert King James Version passages in them, thinking to improve on what Jesus said?

Are we to believe the specious arguments of critics who say that Joseph supposed that he could do better than the prophet Mormon? Did he have either the knowledge or the discretion to determine that the King James translators were superior to the prophet Mormon in the preparation of scriptural texts? Where is their sense of reason?

Mormon was a mature and inspired prophet. Since Joseph was but an unlearned farm boy, how could he improve on Mormon's work?

This young man was faithful to his charge. He did not tamper with the work of Mormon, the sermons of Jesus, the marvelous defense of Abinadi, or the writings of Malachi or

Isaiah. He was strictly a translator, not an editor or a composer; nor was he a thief plagiarizing someone else's work.

The whole task of translation was a miracle. The book is "a marvellous work and a wonder," as Isaiah said. (Isaiah 29:14.)

It was translated in about forty-five working days. That was a miracle itself, and allowed no time for editing, rewriting or Bible research, which would have been required if what the critics say had been true. A book of six hundred pages in forty-five days? The Book of Mormon was a miracle and it remains a miracle!

9

The Bible
Passages

The similarity between parts of the Book of Mormon and the King James translation of the Bible is but a tribute to the accuracy of that version of the Jewish scriptures.

When the King James translators began their work, they did so with fasting and prayer. For the most part they were pious men who sought the inspiration of the Lord in their work. We believe they received it!

How do we know? Because Bible quotations by the Lord and his prophets, as contained in the Book of Mormon, are for the most part almost identical in both volumes of scripture.

The Book of Mormon is a translation, inspired of God from beginning to end. It is true that the Book of Mormon contains many quotations from the Old Testament. They were excerpts from the brass plates of Laban. Hence the brass plates quotations literally were made a part of Mormon's plates, and in turn were translated by Joseph Smith through revelation.

Joseph declared that the Book of Mormon is the most correct book on earth. He would not have said that if he were its author, realizing how poorly educated he was at the time. His complete honesty would have rebelled. He was the translator, and that is all. The Book of Mormon is far beyond any competency that he had at any time in his life, as also are revelations in the Doctrine and Covenants. The answer is that they are from God. They are inspired language, and not in any way the personal product of this young American prophet.

When Joseph was translating the Book of Mormon, he knew so little about the Old Testament that he was in no way capable of taking carefully selected passages from it and putting them into the Book of Mormon, or any other book. Nor could he have added phrases to New Testament passages.

Let us note a few cases in point.

First we turn to the Sermon on the Mount. (The italicized words below show how the Book of Mormon wording differs from that of the book of Matthew.) This unlettered farm laborer would never have thought of making this addition to the Beatitudes:

"Blessed are the poor in spirit *who come unto me*, for theirs is the kingdom of heaven." (3 Nephi 12:3.)

Or this one:

"Blessed are all they who do hunger and thirst after righteousness, for they shall be filled *with the Holy Ghost*. (3 Nephi 12:6.)

Or this one from later on in the Sermon on the Mount:

"Verily, verily, I say unto you, I give unto you to be the light of this people. ["Ye are the light of the world," says Matthew.] A city that is set on a hill cannot be hid." (3 Nephi 12:14.)

And consider this choice one from the twelfth chapter of 3 Nephi and compare it with the fifth chapter of Matthew.

From Matthew: "But I say unto you, That whosoever looketh on a woman to lust after her hath committed adultery with her already in his heart." (Matthew 5:28.)

From 3 Nephi:

"But I say unto you, that whosoever looketh on a woman, to lust after her, hath committed adultery already in his heart. *Behold, I give unto you a commandment, that ye suffer none of these things to enter into your heart; For it is better that ye should deny yourselves of these things, wherein ye will take up your cross, than that ye should be cast into hell."* (3 Nephi 12:28-30.)

Would the unlettered farm boy have thought of "fixing" the Savior's sermon in this manner? Where would he even get such an idea? He was not a scholar of the Bible in the worldly meaning of the word, nor of any other work. And certainly he was not a "man of the cloth."

In chapter 13 of 3 Nephi we have another variation. The Book of Mormon reads: *"Verily, verily, I say unto you that ye should do alms unto the poor;* but take heed that ye do not your alms before men *to be seen of them;* otherwise ye have no reward of your Father *who* is in heaven." (3 Nephi 13:1.)

Matthew has it read: "Take heed that ye do not your alms before men, to be seen of them: otherwise ye have no reward of your Father which is in heaven." (Matthew 6:1.)

Could Joseph Smith have devised such changes in the Savior's divine address? Then why give him credit for something which was far beyond him?

One of the Savior's great sermons to the Nephites is found in chapters 20 and 21 of 3 Nephi. The Savior quotes chapter 54 of Isaiah, much as it appears in the Old Testament.

Can anyone say that Joseph Smith had the ability to make such an alteration? Had he the audacity to do such a thing to the sermon of the Almighty Creator of heaven and earth? Would Joseph have dared tamper with such sacred utterances? Would any conscientious, honest person?

A similar thing is noted as the Savior's sermon appears in chapters 24 and 25 of 3 Nephi. There Malachi is quoted.

Note that Malachi lived some two hundred years after the family of Lehi left Jerusalem en route to America. Therefore, his writings were not in the brass plates of Laban. Hence the Savior quoted them for one good reason — he wanted the Nephites to be acquainted with them. This he said in so many words:

"And now it came to pass that when Jesus had told these things he expounded them unto the multitude; and he did expound all things unto them, both great and small.

"And he saith: These scriptures, which ye had not with you, the Father commanded that I should give unto you: for it was wisdom in him that they should be given unto future generations." (3 Nephi 26:1-2; italics added.)

That alone should answer every critic who says that Joseph purloined parts of the Bible and placed them at convenient places in the Book of Mormon.

The wonderful defense made by Abinadi is a most convincing case in point with respect to this discussion. Any reader of his debate with the priests of King Noah will readily see that it was Abinadi himself who used the Old Testament quotations in his sermon. But they match the language of the Bible!

Read carefully chapters 12, 13 and 14 of Mosiah. Note that the Ten Commandments are given there precisely as they are in the King James version. But did Joseph Smith put them there? Did he devise the dramatic situation in which Abinadi confounded the wicked priests of King Noah with the very quotations from the Old Testament which our present-day critics say Joseph put there? Utterly impossible!

Note also his quotation from the cherished fifty-third chapter of Isaiah. Compare it with the Bible, word for word, and realize that it is a quotation from the brass plates, which were known to Abinadi and correctly quoted by him. These Isaiah passages were part of his sermon, given by him to add emphasis to what he told those wicked priests. His sermon was inscribed by Mormon on the gold plates, passages from the brass plates and all. They then were correctly translated into the modern Book of Mormon by Joseph Smith with the use of the Urim and Thummim. No scholarship (of which there was precious little anyway) of Joseph Smith was involved.

Where is there any sermon more beautiful, coming from any prophet, than that provided by Abinadi as he explains "how beautiful are the feet of them"? (Mosiah 15.)

Read it carefully and know that Joseph Smith never could have produced that bit of literary excellence. Remember that he was an unlearned man at this time, according to his wife and mother, and according to the prophet Isaiah as well. (See Isaiah 29.)

Why are we not willing to accept the whole Book of Mormon as a divine translation? Why does anyone seek to "water down" the work of God, or to humanize it by saying that much of it was the fruit of Joseph's untrained and unlettered brain?

The Book of Mormon is a divinely inspired translation. It is the most correct book on earth. It was not the work of any modern man, farm laborer, scholar or cleric. It came from God.

We say again, the similarity between Bible passages in the Book of Mormon and the Book of Mormon itself is a mighty tribute to the accuracy and inspiration of the King James translation.

The preservation of the Bible through the ages is itself a miracle. It was accomplished only through the hand of God. Then why not its translation? The King James translators did everything they knew how to to obtain divine inspiration for their task. Knowing the great value of that book to the Gentiles, as Nephi himself said, would God withhold the necessary inspiration? Those humble translators were instruments in the hands of the Almighty to further his purpose among the Gentiles. (See 1 Nephi 13.)

10

What Was the Method?

President Joseph Fielding Smith, in his writings, calls attention to the fact that the Prophet Joseph Smith had possession of the plates over a considerable period during which he attempted no translation at all.

He received the plates from the angel Moroni in September of 1827. It was not until April 5, 1829, that Oliver Cowdery came to Joseph's home and agreed to become his scribe. It was two days later that the actual translation was undertaken by these two men.

President Smith says: "We may conclude from the evidence that the actual time of translating the record, as we have it in the Book of Mormon, was between April 7, 1829, and the first week of June of that same year, or not to exceed two full months." (Joseph Fielding Smith, "Translation and Publication of the Book of Mormon," *Improvement Era*, September 1927, page 948.)

The Grandin press began the printing in August, 1829, and the Book of Mormon was ready for distribution about the first of March, 1830. This of course was but a few weeks before the organization of the Church.

President Smith gives us this information:

"Joseph Smith received the plates and the Urim and Thummim September 22, 1827. Because of persecution, poverty, and the necessity of 'laboring with his hands' for a living, nothing was done towards translating the record that year. However, he was busy studying the characters and making himself familiar with them and the use of the Urim and Thummim. He had a great deal more to do than merely to sit down and with the use of the instrument prepared for that purpose translate the characters on the plates. Nothing worth while comes to us merely for the asking. All knowledge and skill are obtained by consistent and determined study and practice, and so the Prophet found it to be the case in the translating of the Book of Mormon. It will be remembered that the Lord said to Oliver Cowdery when he desired to translate: 'But, behold, I say unto you, that you must study it out in your mind.' Oliver thought it would be easy, but found it difficult and therefore was content to accept the advice from the Lord and continue as scribe to Joseph Smith." (Smith, *Improvement Era,* September 1927, page 946.)

There is no record indicating that the Prophet ever described the method of translation. Many have guessed at the procedure, but Joseph himself never described it in writing.

It is presumed that he used the Urim and Thummim occasionally over a period of about two years to study the characters on the plates, and thus became somewhat acquainted with it.

But even so, all was accomplished by revelation. Some descriptions of the process have been published, but they are under considerable question.

11

What Joseph
Did Not Know

When Joseph and Oliver began their work together in translating the Book of Mormon, Joseph was indeed the unlettered man of whom Isaiah spoke.

He had received what would amount to not more than a sixth-grade education at best. It was obtained largely in one- and two-room schools on the frontier of the nation, and then only spasmodically throughout his youth. It was interrupted by removals of the family from one location to another, and by the necessity of the young man to find employment to help support the home.

His teachers were in no way comparable to our educators of today. Their training was at most limited.

Considering these facts, and other related matters as well, the early inadequacy of Joseph Smith as a young man comes strongly into view. He never could have translated the plates in any length of time, let alone the two months in which it was accomplished. Only by divine aid could it have been done, and only by divine aid was it done. It was a miracle from every standpoint.

There is no evidence that Joseph and Oliver translated on the Sabbath day. They were devout worshippers of the Lord.

Take out the Sundays from the translating schedule of two months. Remove also the days when they were forced to change their residence because of persecution.

Of the two months in which they worked, minus those interruptions, it would seem that there may have been only forty to forty-five days spent on the plates! That would mean that they had to produce an average of from ten to fifteen pages of translation every day, a thing from which our skilled modern translators, dealing only with well-known modern languages, would shrink.

Translators today will normally cover about three pages per day when working on a book such as the Book of Mormon.

Think then of the miracle required for these two unskilled young men to translate up to fifteen pages a day from what Moroni called Reformed Egyptian, a language utterly unknown to even the greatest scholars of today. Could it have been anything less than a miracle?

Many are the developments which give corroborative evidence regarding the Book of Mormon, but which have come to light only since that book was published. Joseph Smith knew nothing of those things.

He had never learned in any school about the archaeological wonders of Mexico and Central America. The first books on the subject came more than a decade after the Book of Mormon was off the press.

John L. Stephens, Esq., known as the father of American archaeology, published *Incidents of Travel in Central America, Chiapas and Yucatan* in 1841. Two years later he produced *Incidents of Travel in Yucatan*. It is recorded that when these books finally came west, Joseph Smith did obtain copies and read them.

Stephens, accompanied by Frederick Catherwood who made drawings of the wonders they beheld, made the trip through many of the ruined areas. There were no excavations in those days, of course, but there were many remains of grandeur which they did see as they explored the jungles. Catherwood sketched them, Stephens described them, and their book was widely circulated. Between 1841 and 1871 Harper's published twelve editions of the Stephens book. But in 1829 the book was nonexistent; the explorers had not yet made their trip. So Joseph knew nothing of what these men were to find ten or more years after the Book of Mormon was printed.

Before Stephens, there was no accurate description of any Mayan city. So like all other Americans, Joseph was not informed on this subject either.

The young prophet did not know that the ancient Americans were well versed in astronomy, and that they had produced a calendar as accurate as that which we used today. How could he have known? And yet, the Book of Mormon indicates that the ancients were acquainted with the movement of the planets and lived by them. Joseph knew nothing about such intricacies of astronomy.

Until Moroni came, Joseph was not acquainted with gold or any other metallic plates on which ancient records were made. He had no idea that archaeologists would subsequently find such plates in a hundred different locations, from Java to Spain and from the Near East to Mexico.

Joseph was unaware of the pyramids in America which rival the pyramids of Egypt.

He had not learned that in ancient times, both white men and dark men lived in America, and that some of them had gone to the Polynesian Islands where they were seen by Captain Cook and others.

He did not know that the Inca rulers were white men with white wives and that they preserved the white race for royalty. This led to much inbreeding which later weakened these families.

He was not informed about American Indians' traditions telling of their original forefathers having come to American shores on a boat — that there were four brothers who were white and wore beards.

He had never been taught that among the natives on Easter Island were white men, some of them six and a half feet tall. The Spanish explorers who saw them said that these white men had blond or red hair and that they were greatly respected.

He had not heard that there was a tradition of the coming of a White God, and that this legend is found in nearly all tribes of American Indians, and in the Polynesian islands as far south as New Zealand.

This White God wore flowing white robes, and his face was white and shining like the sun. He taught the people many things to help them to live better. He performed many miracles among them, and promised that he would come again. But Joseph had never heard of him!

Joseph did not know that this tradition led to the downfall of Montezuma and his people of Mexico in the time of Cortez, with a similar condition in South America involving Pizarro. He did not know that when Captain Cook, a white man, arrived in the Hawaiian islands in his white-sailed ship, he was greeted by the natives as the returning White God.

He did not know that the Polynesians believed that their forefathers came from the far west, from a land of very high mountains, and that before this, their ancestors came from over other and more distant waters.

He knew nothing of the Hebrew language in those days, and yet his book is filled with Hebrew idioms. He knew nothing of the names that later became well known to American explorers, names which appear in both the Book of Mormon and in tribal tradition.

Here is another point. Would any sixth grader dream up a situation indicating that "the land northward" was so short of timber that they imported lumber from the "land southward," with the cargo being carried in sea-going ships?

Would a person of meager education, who probably never had so much as seen the ocean at that time of his life, have provided information about a sea-going lumber trade being carried on between the two lands, one southward and the other northward? How could he know about sea-going ships? He certainly had never seen one, not to mention having set foot on one.

Could he have imagined a lumber shortage which would bring about a boom in the use of cement? There is no archaeological evidence about the timber portion of this discussion since wood decomposes so quickly, but there is ample evidence of the extensive use of cement two thousand years ago in the areas of ancient America, both north and south.

How could Joseph have known? No unlettered youth could have written such a thing as this:

"And now no part of the land was desolate, save it were for timber; but because of the greatness of the destruction of the people who had before inhabited the land it was called desolate.

"And there being but little timber upon the face of the land, nevertheless the people who went forth became exceeding expert in the working of cement; therefore they did build houses of cement, in the which they did dwell.

"And it came to pass that they did multiply and spread, and did go forth from the land southward to the land northward, and did spread insomuch that they began to cover the face of the whole earth, from the sea south to the sea north, from the sea west to the sea east.

"And the people who were in the land northward did dwell in tents, and in houses of cement, and they did suffer whatsoever tree should spring up upon the face of the land that it should grow up, that in time they might have timber to build their houses, yea, their cities, and their temples, and their synagogues, and their sanctuaries, and all manner of their buildings.

"And it came to pass as timber was exceeding scarce in the land northward, they did send forth much by the way of shipping.

"And thus they did enable the people in the land northward that they might build many cities, both of wood and of cement.

"And it came to pass that there were many of the people of Ammon, who were Lamanites by birth, did also go forth into this land.

"And now there are many records kept of the proceedings of this people, by many of this people, which are particular and very large, concerning them.

"But behold, a hundredth part of the proceedings of this people, yea, the account of the Lamanites and of the Nephites, and their wars, and contentions, and dissensions, and their preaching, and their prophecies, *and their shipping and their building of ships, and their building of temples,* and of synagogues and their sanctuaries, and their righteousness, and their wickedness, and their murders, and their robbings, and their plundering, and all manner of abominations and whoredoms, cannot be contained in this work." (Helaman 3:6-14; italics added.)

There were hosts of things Joseph Smith did not know before his work of translation — many of them mentioned in the Book of Mormon. They could be brought forth by him only through a miracle.

What Joseph did not know becomes one of the most important corroborative phases of the entire Book of Mormon study. Many important things were in the book, having been written there by the authors, Mormon and his son Moroni. But to Joseph Smith, before the translation, they were unknown.

12

More Peculiarities

If Joseph Smith, an unlettered frontier farm laborer, had written the Book of Mormon out of his own wisdom, how would he have arrived at personal and place names that appear in the volume?

Dr. Hugh Nibley of the BYU, in his book *Lehi in the Desert and the World of the Jaredites,* mentions a long list of such names.

In western New York in 1829, information concerning such names was simply not available, either to scholars or farmers. And certainly they were not within the meager educational reach of Joseph Smith.

Note just a few taken at random from the list provided by Dr. Nibley:

Aha was the name of the son of a Nephite commander. It was also the name of the first pharaoh in Egypt and means "warrior."

Ammon, well known in the Book of Mormon, was also commonly used in Egypt.

Hem, the brother of the Nephite Ammon. This was also the name of the high priest of Thebes.

Helaman, Nephite prophet. The name Heramon, so much like it, was the Egyptian form.

Himni was the son of Mosiah. Hmn was the Egyptian hawk-god, symbol of the emperor.

Korihor, enemy of the Saints; Kherihor was an Egyptian high priest in 1085 B.C.

Paanchi was the son of Pahoran, Nephite judge; Paanchi was also a high priest at Thebes.

Pahoran was a Nephite chief judge. Paheron was ambassador of Egypt to Palestine.

Manti was a Nephite city. Manti is the Semitic form of an Egyptian proper name.

Pacumeni was a son of the Nephite chief judge; Pakamen was the high priest of Horus in Egypt.

Pachus of the Book of Mormon resembles Pachqs, an Egyptian proper name.

Zenock was a prophet; Zenekh was an Egyptian proper name.

When it is recalled that the Book of Mormon was written in Reformed Egyptian, it would be most unlikely if many names in that book were not also related to Egypt.

But Joseph at this early time in his life knew no Egyptian; he knew no other language either, for that matter. In and of himself he was in no way capable of dreaming up names that had legitimate Egyptian connections.

The story of the flood of Noah's day is known among nearly all ancient peoples. It is given only as a legend by the scholars, but the account, in its various local versions, is nevertheless there.

The Babylonian account says that the inside of the ark was lighted by shining stones. This legend is paralleled by a Jewish tradition attributed to Rabbi Ahia ben Zeira, who wrote, in connection with the Talmud, that "in the midst of the darkness of the ark, Noah distinguished day from night by aid of pearl and precious stones whose lustre turned pale in the daylight and glittered at night."

Joseph Smith wrote that the brother of Jared placed stones before the Lord, who touched them and they became luminous. These stones were used to light the barges for the Jaredites.

Could an unlettered farm boy on the western frontier of the United States have known about the Babylonian and Jewish traditions, which even now, in this enlightened age, are known to very few people? Could he have dreamed up the situation in which these stones of the Jaredites were touched by the finger of the Lord? And could he have devised the situation following this episode in which the Lord himself appeared? Why are not the critics a bit realistic?

There are also references to astronomy in the Book of Mormon, which are most interesting in view of Joseph's meager sixth-grade background.

In Joseph's day were there still people who were not sure whether the world was flat or round? That is so. Were there still uninformed ones that knew very little about the motion of planets? That also is so. Joseph certainly was in no way equipped to discuss astronomy. And yet, we have these verses in the Book of Mormon:

"For the stars of heaven and the constellations thereof shall not give their light; the sun shall be darkened in her going forth, and the moon shall not cause her light to shine." (2 Nephi 23:10.)

"But Alma said unto him: Thou hast had signs enough; will ye tempt your God? Will ye say, Show unto me a sign, when ye have the testimony of all these thy brethren, and also all the holy prophets? The scriptures are laid before thee, yea, and all things denote there is a God; yea, even the earth, and all things that are upon the face of it, yea, and its motion, yea, and also all the planets which move in their regular form do witness that there is a Supreme Creator." (Alma 30:44.)

"And thus, according to his word the earth goeth back, and it appeareth unto man that the sun standeth still; yea, and behold, this is so; for surely it is the earth that moveth and not the sun." (Helaman 12:15.)

Could an unlearned farmer have written those words?

And then there is the literary style of the Book of Mormon, and the sheer beauty of many of its passages. Consider again the sermon of Abinadi.

"Yea, and are not the prophets, every one that has opened his mouth to prophesy, that has not fallen into transgression,

I mean all the holy prophets ever since the world began? I say unto you that they are his seed.

"And these are they who have published peace, who have brought good tidings of good, who have published salvation; and said unto Zion: Thy God reigneth!

"And O how beautiful upon the mountains were their feet!

"And again, how beautiful upon the mountains are the feet of those that are still publishing peace!

"And again, how beautiful upon the mountains are the feet of those who shall hereafter publish peace, yea, from this time henceforth and forever!

"And behold, I say unto you, this is not all. For O how beautiful upon the mountains are the feet of him that bringeth good tidings, that is the founder of peace, yea, even the Lord, who has redeemed his people; yea, him who has granted salvation unto his people;

"For were it not for the redemption which he hath made for his people, which was prepared from the foundation of the world, I say unto you, were it not for this, all mankind must have perished." (Mosiah 15:13-19.)

Consider Mormon's dissertation on infant baptism. What scholar even today could match it? Read it in Moroni, chapter 8. And what of King Benjamin's marvelous address? It is a classic if ever there was one.

Could Joseph Smith have imagined the situation wherein the Lord administered the sacrament of the Lord's Supper to the multitude, with the emblems being provided miraculously?

Would he have imagined the appointment and subsequent experiences of the three Nephites?

Could he as a sixth grader have drawn from his imagination the eleventh chapter of 3 Nephi describing the coming of the Savior to ancient America?

One of the most difficult things for the critics to explain is the revelation giving advance information on the establishment of the United States, as set forth in the Book of Mormon.

The Savior had said this:

"For it is wisdom in the Father that they should be established in this land, and be set up as a free people by the power of the Father, that these things might come forth from them unto a remnant of your seed, that the covenant of the Father may be fulfilled which he hath covenanted with his people, O house of Israel." (3 Nephi 21:4.)

And Nephi saw this:

"And I looked and beheld a man among the Gentiles, who was separated from the seed of my brethren by the many waters; and I beheld the Spirit of God, that it came down and wrought upon the man; and he went forth upon the many waters, even unto the seed of my brethren, who were in the promised land.

"And it came to pass that I beheld the Spirit of God, that it wrought upon other Gentiles; and they went forth out of captivity, upon the many waters.

"And it came to pass that I beheld many multitudes of the Gentiles upon the land of promise; and I beheld the wrath of God, that it was upon the seed of my brethren; and they were scattered before the Gentiles and were smitten.

"And I beheld the Spirit of the Lord, that it was upon the Gentiles, and they did prosper and obtain the land for their inheritance; and I beheld that they were white, and exceeding fair and beautiful, like unto my people before they were slain.

"And it came to pass that I, Nephi, beheld that the Gentiles who had gone forth out of captivity did humble themselves before the Lord; and the power of the Lord was with them.

"And I beheld that their mother Gentiles were gathered together upon the waters, and upon the land also, to battle against them.

"And I beheld that the power of God was with them, and also that the wrath of God was upon all those that were gathered together against them to battle.

"And I, Nephi, beheld that the Gentiles that had gone out of captivity were delivered by the power of God out of the hands of all other nations." (1 Nephi 13:12-19.)

Joseph neither imagined these things, nor did he copy them out of the Bible, for of course they are not in that volume. Yet they are prophecies which have come true! History vindicates Joseph Smith in this important respect as it also vindicates the Book of Mormon. Only an inspired volume could give information on the establishment of the United States more than two thousand years in advance of the events.

When we speak of what Joseph did not know, and admit that this condition corroborates the Book of Mormon, it is interesting to note that he could have known none of the things mentioned in this chapter. They all came through the translation of what to him was an unknown book. It was sheer revelation.

13

The Timing of Prophecy

When Isaiah spoke of the coming forth of the Book of Mormon, as we read it in the twenty-ninth chapter of his book, he provided time limits within which his prediction would come true.

He spoke of the words of a sacred book which would be given to a learned man, saying, "Read this, I pray thee: and he saith, I cannot; for it is sealed:

"And the book is delivered to him that is not learned, saying, Read this, I pray thee: and he saith, I am not learned."

Then through his prophet the Lord says: "Behold, I will proceed to do a marvellous work among this people, even a marvellous work and a wonder."

The scripture follows with these crucial and fateful words:

"Is it not yet a very little while, and Lebanon shall be turned into a fruitful field, and the fruitful field shall be esteemed as a forest?

"And in that day shall the deaf hear the words of the book, and the eyes of the blind shall see out of obscurity, and out of darkness." (Isaiah 29:11-12, 14, 17-18.)

The prophecy goes further, but the point we make here is the timing Isaiah established for the coming forth of this miracle book which should be so important even to the blind and deaf.

He says specifically that the book should come forth before Palestine again becomes a fruitful field. Note the language again. He tells of the coming forth of the book, and then says: "Is it not yet a very little while, and Lebanon shall be turned into a fruitful field, and the fruitful field shall be esteemed as a forest?"

That is significant.

Palestine had been a desert for centuries before 1830 when the Book of Mormon was published. It continued to be a desert until a half a century ago when the migrating Jews reclaimed it and made the desert literally bloom as a fruitful field.

When did the resettlement of the Jews begin? Only after British General Allenby liberated the area from the Turks in 1917, near the end of the First World War.

There was neither resettlement of the Jews nor any tilling of the land before that date. But during the ensuing years, a marvelous thing happened. The lands are fruitful now, beyond belief. And the forests spoken of by the prophet? Millions upon millions of trees have been planted there in the last half century, trees for timber, trees for watersheds, and trees for orchards, miles and miles of them.

Even the valley of Armageddon abundantly produces grapes, peaches, and oranges.

The book came out on time. The prophecy was fulfilled. Again Joseph Smith is vindicated.

Does anyone suppose that all by himself he contrived some way to fulfil Isaiah's twenty-ninth chapter? Not only would he have had to produce the book itself, but he would have had to arrange for the resettlement of Palestine by people dogged enough to reclaim the desert and make it a fruitful land, even providing a big export business for the Jews.

Is it not all a marvelous work and a wonder? A miracle? A manifestation of the hand of God? A warning that the end is drawing near?

14

Polynesians and Indians

Latter-day Saints believe that the Polynesians are descendants of Lehi and blood relatives of the American Indians. For that reason, from the beginning of our Church history we have had more than an ordinary interest in them as a people.

But now that interest is even more keen. Recent research on the part of world-recognized scientists and scholars has focused a new light upon them and writings of early explorers in both America and Polynesia have become available now for detailed study.

The new knowledge which has been developed shows that, without any reasonable doubt, the Polynesians came from America, that they are closely related to the American Indians in many respects, and that even their traditions and genealogies bear that out.

So pronounced is this feeling among some world scholars of today that one of them, Thor Heyerdahl, the widely known Norwegian anthropologist who sailed the raft *Kon Tiki* from America to the Polynesian islands, titled one of his books, *American Indians in the Pacific*. It is a remarkable volume of great interest to Latter-day Saints.

With him are other writers who confirm and reconfirm the

facts now being disclosed that there is strong reason to believe that the Polynesians are directly related to the American Indians, and that they came from American shores. They sailed westward to their Pacific islands, taking with them their customs, their food, and their religion, all of which have left a permanent mark upon Polynesia.

Pronounced as are these views establishing the relationship of Polynesians and American Indians, there are equally impressive data now available to disprove the theory that the Polynesians originated in the Orient and came eastward from Indonesia, Malaya, and nearby lands. Let us just mention a few of the convincing points of evidence.

Many have seen the great stone pyramids, or photographs of them, discovered by archaeologists in Mexico, Central and South America. Pyramids of almost identical structure, both in plan and material, if not in size, have been found in Polynesia.

Stone roadways, so characteristic of the pre-Inca period of America, are found to be duplicated in some of the Pacific islands. Giant stone statues such as are found in the lands of the South American Incas, are now discovered in the Polynesian islands, with characteristics and markings so similar that few can doubt their common origin. This includes many of the structures found on Easter Island.

The sweet potato of the Pacific islands, known in Polynesia as the *kumara* (or *kumalla*, as it is called in Tonga), is now found by botanists to be the identical plant which is native to South America, with impressive evidence as to the manner in which it was transported from Peru to the Pacific islands.

Cotton, coconuts, pineapples, and papaya are likewise being traced from Polynesia to America by botanists who now announce that the Polynesian varieties of these plants are but offshoots of the parent plants in America.

The ocean currents have been observed in our time to carry drifting objects to Polynesia from two places in America, one being the Pacific Northwest and the other the Central and South American region. Large Pacific Northwest pine logs have been traced in the drifting currents of the Pacific Ocean from the Vancouver area of North America to the Hawaiian,

Marshall, and Caroline islands. Hawaiians and other Polynesians have made canoes from these drifted pine logs and in them have traveled from island to island. There are no such trees growing in Polynesia. They came by ocean currents from the Pacific Northwest of America.

This is even more notable when it is observed that customs and household articles characteristic of the Indians of the Pacific Northwest of America have been found on a wide scale in Polynesia.

Written descriptions of fortifications built on some of the Polynesian islands remind one of chapters in the Book of Mormon which portray the fortifications built by the great general Moroni here in ancient America. Kivas, characteristic of American Indian cultures, are found in Polynesia.

Words and place names in the language of the Polynesians of the various island groups are now found to be identical to those common among the Inca people of Peru. Many of these words are actually identical in spelling and pronunciation.

One of them is *Kanakana,* the name of one of the deities of both the Incas and the Polynesians. It means brightness or light or knowledge or intelligence. They believed that the glory of their God was intelligence and therefore named him so. This is noted in both pre-Inca and Polynesian religions.

There are many other religious teachings which are the same in both areas. Both people believe in the creation by the Almighty. They both believe that the first man was the father of all living and that the first woman was the mother of all living, using these actual phrases. They believe in the flood of Noah's day. They accept an atonement by a Savior. They both believe in a White God who came among their forefathers and performed mighty miracles. They believe in the water of life, or living water, which is given by the Savior.

The islanders say that their forefathers came from the east, from a land of high mountains and plateaus in the skies, which fits the description of the western coast of South America. Genealogies of the Pacific islanders are traced to American ancestors.

Structures which archaeologists claim were baptismal fonts have been found in both areas. Burial customs are similar. Both groups believed in an all-powerful governing trinity of Gods. There is one story in Polynesia which reminds us of the story of the brother of Jared.

One of the most interesting of all the reports brought out by Heyerdahl and other scientists who have made a serious study of the Polynesians and their relationship to the Americans is this:

Anthropologists have learned that prior to the coming of the Spaniards, there were both white and brown people in America, that the white people were as white as snow, according to their descriptions, and that they had brown, blonde, or red hair. The hair was not dyed or treated in any way. It grew that way. Heyerdahl has photographic proof, showing mummies as examples.

They tell us also that white people as well as brown people emigrated from America to Polynesia and that some of these white people lived in the islands in the times of the early explorers in the Pacific, who saw them and wrote about them. Think of the significance of this fact in relation to the Book of Mormon! These white men living in the islands wore beards and their faces resembled those of Europeans.

Such white people actually were seen on Easter Island, as well as on other Pacific islands, and although they no longer survive, the traditions of the natives tell of them, as do the authentic writings of early historians.

On Easter Island, Heyerdahl himself was told by the mayor of the principal community that there were two kinds of people on that island at first, white and brown, and that the white people were really white, with light-colored hair. The anthropologists have long since discarded the idea that they might have been albinos.

Captain Cook saw some of these white natives on his journeys and wrote about them. One came aboard his ship. The other natives told Captain Cook that this white native was their leader, that he was of divine descent, and that he was therefore held in high respect.

It is notable that the highest ideal of beauty among these islanders was the white skin. It was regarded as a sign of descent from the best of the ancient lineages and as a symbol of chieftainship of pure blood.

But where did these white people come from and how did

they reach these islands? Evidence recently compiled indicates that they came from America.

But were there white men in early America, previous to the coming of the Spaniards? Recently published records tell about similar white people found in Peru. Pedro Pizarro, cousin to Francisco Pizarro and chronicler of the Spanish conquerors, wrote that whereas the majority of the Indians in the Andes Mountains were small and of brown complexion, the members of the ruling family were tall and had whiter skins than the Spaniards themselves. Pizarro says that these white Incas of Peru actually were white, not albinos, but white people with soft blonde or brown or red hair.

Archaeologists have now found mummies of the Inca period bearing out this fact. Colored photographs of well-preserved mummies, with soft blonde or red or brown hair, have been published and widely distributed.

Pizarro asked the Incas of his day who these white people were and was told that they were the last of the descendants of a divine race of white men with beards. These men were given the name of Viracocha, or "sea foam," because they were so white.

We live today in a time of research, discovery, and knowledge. The new knowledge bears testimony that both Nephites and Lamanites lived in ancient America. Regardless of the names given them by the scientists or the early Incas, to us they were Nephites and Lamanites. This new knowledge likewise bears testimony that both Nephites and Lamanites emigrated from America to Polynesia, that they have been seen by explorers and seafarers who have written about them and that their customs and beliefs relate to the Book of Mormon.

15

The Great
White God

The ancient Americans were a truly great and progressive people. Dr. Alfred V. Kidder, one of the leading authorities on the Mayan culture, wrote in his book *A Guide to Quirigua:*

"The great cities of the old Mayan Empire were built during the first part of the Christian era. For nearly 600 years these gifted people were leaders in art and architecture, mathematics and astronomy. They evolved a calendar in some ways more accurate than ours.... The growth of the Indian civilizations, although differing in detail, was strikingly like that of our own, which originated in Egypt and Mesopotamia.... Social and economic systems were organized, cities grew, religion developed, and temples were built for worship."

Writing in a similar vein, in his book *The Marvels of Copan*, the historian Munoz wrote: "Architecture, astronomy, mathematics, painting, weaving and all the arts that embellish life, once flourished here."

He emphasized that the forefathers of the Indian were not savages in any sense, for no savage, he said, ever conceived of the wonders which were commonly known among the Mayans.

The Mayans, through a process similar to that used by the Egyptians, manufactured a paper-like writing material from papyrus.

In *The American Heritage Book of Indians* we read:

"The Mayas attained the highest civilization known in ancient America, and one of the highest known anyplace in the early world." (Alvin M. Josephy, Jr., ed., *The American Heritage Book of Indians* [American Heritage Publishing Co., Inc., 1961], page 19.)

These people had a well-developed irrigation system. They built dams and aqueducts. They terraced hillsides, turning them into productive farm lands by the use of irrigation. Some of these water systems, in general use two thousand years before the Spaniards came, still exist.

The early Americans were a numerous people. About the time of the Spanish conquest there were 25 million in Central Mexico alone.

But more impressive than any of these facts about the early Americans is their account of a visitation among their ancestors nearly two thousand years ago of a Divine Personage who remained among them for many days, teaching and blessing them.

These highly intelligent and skillful early Americans affirmed that this Personage taught them a divine religion, healed their sick, raised some of the dead, taught new and more productive agricultural methods and established a government of equity and peace.

Their accounts say that he came among them suddenly and left equally so, in a supernatural manner. The ancients regarded him as the Creator, come to earth in bodily form.

That his teachings were akin to the Bible is now readily admitted.

And that he promised to return in a second coming is also an acknowledged fact.

The account of his appearance was preserved through generations of Indians from Chile to Alaska, and, interestingly enough, it is likewise well known among the Polynesians from Hawaii to New Zealand, giving one more evidence of the close relationship between the Polynesians and the early inhabitants of the Americas.

In the main all such accounts agree. They differ in name and minor details from island to island and from country to country, but the overall conclusion is the same — there was a visitation by a Heavenly Being among those people nearly two thousand years ago.

Of such veracity is the information now available concerning him that Paul Herrmann was induced to say in his book *Conquest by Man:*

"Carefully considered this leaves no conclusion open than that the Light God Quetzalcoatl was a real person, that he was neither an invention of Spanish propaganda nor a legendary figment of Indian imagination." (Paul Herrmann, *Conquest by Man* [New York: Harper & Brothers, 1954], page 172.)

Keep in mind that this comes from the highly intelligent early Americans who knew astronomy, mathematics, irrigation and architecture. It was not the dream of an ignorant or superstitious people. It was history from one of the highest civilizations known among ancient men.

This great Being was known as Quetzalcoatl in parts of Mexico, primarily in the Cholula area. He was Votan in Chiapas, Wixepechocha in Oaxaca, Gucumatz in Guatemala, Virachocha and Hyustus in Peru, Sume in Brazil, and Bochica in Colombia.

To the Peruvians he was also known as Con-tici or Illa-tici, Tici meaning both creator and light. To the Mayans he was principally known as Kukulcan.

In the Polynesian islands he was known as Lono, Kana, Kane, or Kon, and sometimes as Kanaloa — meaning the great Light or great Brightness. He was also known among some Polynesians as Kane-Akea, the Great Progenitor, or as Tonga-roa, the god of the ocean sun.

What did he look like, this Divine Personage?

He was described by the ancients as a tall white man, bearded, and having blue eyes. He wore loose flowing robes. He seemed to be a Person of great authority and unmeasured kindness. He had power to make hills into plains and plains into high mountains. He could bring fountains of water from the solid rock.

One of the remarkable things about his coming was that he appeared after several days of dense darkness during which the people had prayed constantly for a return of the sun. While the darkness yet prevailed, says the book *The Incas of Pedro de Cieza de León,* the people suffered great hardships and offered earnest prayers to God seeking a return of the light that had failed.

When at last the sun did shine, this Divinity appeared. Says Pedro de León: He was a "white man, large of stature, whose air and person aroused great respect and veneration. . . . And when they saw his power, they called him the Maker of all things, their Beginning, Father of the sun." (Victor Wolfgang von Hagen, ed., *The Incas of Pedro de Cieza de León* [Norman, Oklahoma: University of Oklahoma Press, 1959], page 27.)

This Personage, as he taught his religion, urged the people to build temples for worship, and his followers became very devout. (See Pierre Honoré, *In Quest of the White God.*) As he left them he promised to come again, which caused the natives for many generations to look for his return even as the Jews look for their promised Messiah.

This faith led to disaster on two occasions, however, when the Spaniards came to America and when Captain Cook sailed to the Hawaiian Islands. But these tragedies served only to reinforce the truth of the tradition.

When Cortez came to Mexico and the coastal natives saw him, they observed that he was a large white man. They hurried to their king, Montezuma, and announced that the Great White God had finally returned.

This had a striking effect upon Montezuma. He remembered that when he was crowned as emperor, the priests of the native religion reminded him: "This is not your throne, . . . it is only lent to you and will one day be returned to the one to whom it is due." (Pierre Honoré, *In Quest of the White God* [New York: G. P. Putnam's Sons, 1964], pages 66-67.)

The Spanish author Durán, in his book *The Aztecs* says that when Montezuma sent his faithful servant to greet Cortez and lead him to the palace, the servant addressed Cortez as "O lord and true god!" and added, "Welcome to this, your country and kingdom!" Durán further says that the Indians considered Cortez's companions as divine beings also.

Durán also notes:

"There is no doubt that Montezuma was greatly preoccupied with the return of Quetzalcoatl... who had abandoned the Veracruz coast and had promised to return. Eventually, Montezuma and the other dignitaries [of his kingdom] as can be seen in the chronicles, were to become totally convinced that Cortez and Quetzalcoatl were one.... As late as 1864 when the blond, bearded Emperor Maximilian arrived in Veracruz, ... reminiscences lingered in the minds of the Indians which reminded them of the promised return of Quetzalcoatl." (Diego Durán, *The Aztecs* [New York: Orion Press, 1964], pages 278, 354.)

Montezuma accepted Cortez as though he were Deity, but the treachery of the Spaniards and his men soon changed that, and warfare resulted. Poor, trusting Montezuma lost both his throne and his life, but the tradition remained.

A similar situation occurred when Captain James Cook, the British explorer, came to Hawaii. Peculiarly enough, he landed there when the natives were celebrating their Makahiki Festival, which kept alive the tradition of the White God among the Polynesians. Cook also was received as Deity, and taken to the sacred temple of Lono. But his men were far from angelic, and their depredations brought down the wrath of the natives upon the entire landing party. In the battle which ensued, Cook lost his life.

But in reality, who was the Great White God? It was not Captain Cook, and certainly it was not Cortez. Who was he?

When Jesus Christ ministered in Palestine, he told the people there, as is recorded in the tenth chapter of the Gospel of John, that he had other sheep, not of the fold of Palestine, but elsewhere. "Them also I must bring, and they shall hear my voice; and there shall be one fold, and one shepherd." (John 10:16.)

Jesus of Nazareth was this White God! After his resurrection in the Holy Land he did in reality visit the early Americans. How do we know?

In the Western Hemisphere, as in ancient Palestine, prophets ministered among the people, giving them inspired direction. As did the prophets in the Holy Land, they also compiled records of all important events.

They had predicted the coming of Christ among them, and the people fully expected him.

After the three days of darkness which had afflicted them, the people were gathered about their temple when they heard a voice from heaven which said:

"Behold my Beloved Son, in whom I am well pleased, in whom I have glorified my name — hear ye him."

This caused them to look into the skies, and there they saw descending to the earth a glorious Personage, who came and stood before them. And as the ancient volume records it:

"He was clothed in a white robe; and he came down and stood in the midst of them; and the eyes of the whole multitude were turned upon him, and they durst not open their mouths, even one to another. . . .

"And it came to pass that he stretched forth his hand and spake unto the people, saying:

"Behold, I am Jesus Christ, whom the prophets testified shall come into the world.

"And behold, I am the light and the life of the world; and I have drunk out of that bitter cup which the Father hath given me, and have glorified the Father in taking upon me the sins of the world. . . ."

Then the Savior said to them:

"Arise and come forth unto me, that ye may thrust your hands into my side, and also that ye may feel the prints of the nails in my hands and in my feet, that ye may know that I am the God of Israel, and the God of the whole earth, and have been slain for the sins of the world.

"And it came to pass that the multitude went forth, and thrust their hands into his side, and did feel the prints of the nails in his hands and in his feet; and this they did do, going forth one by one until they had all gone forth, and did see with their eyes and did feel with their hands, and did know of a surety and did bear record, that it was he, of whom it was written by the prophets, that should come.

"And when they had all gone forth and had witnessed for themselves, they did cry out with one accord, saying:

"Hosannah! Blessed be the name of the Most High God! And they did fall down at the feet of Jesus and did worship him." (3 Nephi 11:7-11, 14-17.)

He taught them his true religion, healed their sick, blessed their children, and organized his Church on the Western Hemisphere as he had done in Palestine.

This is what gave rise to the tradition of the Indians and Polynesians concerning the return of the White God. And it has lived until now, being transmitted from generation to generation.

16

The Yaqui Story

Existence of a quorum of twelve apostles among the Yaqui Indians of Mexico in modern times, apostles declared by those Indians to be the successors to the first such quorum set apart by the Messiah during a visit made by him on the American continent many generations ago, is made known in the testimony of Ammon M. Tenney, one of the courageous men earlier called by President Brigham Young as an exploring and colonizing missionary.

(Ammon Tenney was a close associate of Jacob Hamblin as a missionary to the Indians. For years he was in charge of the Indian mission in New Mexico. In 1888 he was called to serve a mission among the Mexicans along the Mexican border. In 1890 he was called to help the Mormon colonization of Mexico. He spoke Spanish and several of the Indian dialects, and was used extensively as an interpreter.)

Elder Tenney made a personal visit among those Indians in 1920 and found there a form of worship distinctly Christian, and according to the Indians themselves, antedating the padres who came during the conquest. This form of worship, the Indians told Elder Tenney, was given them during the personal visit of Jesus Christ among their forefathers, when he also ordained the twelve apostles among them.

The story of Elder Tenney's visit among those people was related to LeRoi C. Snow, and was published as a news dispatch in the semi-weekly issue of the *Deseret News,* Thursday, February 10, 1921. The following account of that visit is a summary of that article.

"My special purpose in going into Mexico was to visit the nation of Yaqui Indians, to become acquainted with them, learn direct something about their religion, to do some missionary work among them and to see what the opportunity might be for colonization in their beautiful country.

"I was in Mexico nearly four weeks. I carried with me letters of introduction and recommendation from the governor of Arizona, the Arizona historian and the attorney general. These letters were my passports and opened the way wherever I went.

"I had long desired to visit the Yaqui Indians in their mountain and forest homes in Sonora, for they are so different from all other American Indians.

"I entered Mexico at Nogales, and called on Governor Flavio Borgues, who, after reading my letters of introduction, appointed a guide to accompany me, and gave me freedom to go where I pleased.

"I traveled 150 miles up the Yaqui river, about as far as it is possible to go because of the dense forests. From Hermosilla I went by train to Vicam Switch, was ferried across the river to the old town of Vicam, and made two visits to Potam, both the old and the new town. The Catholic Church is building a very fine cathedral for the Yaqui Indians there. The state religion is Catholic, in fact all the outward and public worship is Catholic, but the natives have a sacred tradition and worship which they practice in secret, and which is much older than their first acquaintance with the Catholic religion.

"Perhaps the greatest surprise to me was to learn that these people actually have a quorum of twelve apostles which was organized among them by the Savior himself and which has been kept fully organized since his appearance, as they claim.

"They say he instructed them to fill vacancies as they

occurred, which they have done. They also crucify the Savior in effigy upon certain occasions as a teaching and lesson to the children. A full-sized figure is made of paper, wood, etc., and then it is crucified publicly before the people.

"What impressed me most was that they claim most earnestly that all this, and more, was given them during a personal visit of Jesus Christ among them. I asked them if they did not get these teachings from the early Spanish fathers, and argued that it must have come from the Catholic monks who came with Cortez and later. The companion who was with me said no, that Cortez and his people did not come among them and that their religion was much older than the days of Cortez and he would prove it.

"My friend told me that the Catholics, as we know, claim a succession from Peter, and that if this people had received their religion from the Catholics they would claim the same, but they do not.

"They claim that it came direct from a visit of the Savior; that he organized the apostles among them, and told them of his crucifixion and that he also taught them the gospel, which was soon accepted by all the people throughout the land, and they all became united and one great people. This was when the apostles were chosen, and the teachings given them which they were still following when the first padres came.

"My companion told me that the Yaquis were a very powerful nation when Cortez made his conquests, and when he approached their borders he heard of their strength and decided he could not conquer them, and turned aside, and neither he nor any of his monks came among them.

"During my short visit I saw some of the twelve apostles, was told that they are held in great respect, and that they are very particular to keep the quorum fully organized. When I again suggested that this might have come from the Catholic monks, my friend said:

" 'The Catholic church does not have the apostles, and would not have appointed them among us. Then, I repeat, the early Spanish explorers did not come among us. We were a powerful nation, and even Montezuma did not dare touch us. The nature of our country, with dense forests of timber, prickly pear and cactus, was so impenetrable and such a strong barrier, that strangers to our country could not get to us.'

"Here my companion marked out more accurately than I could have done, the course taken by the early Spanish explorers, and proved to my entire satisfaction that when they approached the borders of this interesting Yaqui country they turned aside.

"Then my guide continued:

" 'Wherever those early explorers went they left their marks, they built peculiar houses, built missions for their monks, the padres, and left many other signs which can easily be traced along their trails through New Mexico, Arizona, California and many parts of Mexico.'

"He asked me if all this were not so, and, of course, I readily admitted that it was. Then, with much satisfaction, he added:

" 'You do not find one of these ruins on our soil. There are no such signs. Those people were not among us. The twelve apostles, the crucifixion, and other Christian teachings and practices did not come from the Spanish fathers, but it was given us by Christ himself.' "

17

Evidence of Things Not Seen

Some people continue to challenge the Book of Mormon. Not only do they attack the authenticity of that sacred volume, but they question our right to have scriptures other than the Bible.

We Latter-day Saints have three volumes of scripture in addition to the Bible. They are additional witnesses for the Lord Jesus Christ, declaring to all who are willing to read them that he is our Savior and our Redeemer. In this day of trouble and doubt, should we not be grateful for increased affirmations of the Christ?

Having been taught that the Bible contains all of the word of God, some ask us why we have these other scriptures. They do not realize that the Bible provides for more scripture and that it points to a pattern established anciently by the Lord in which he placed prophets on earth to provide that scripture.

Their revelations were recorded, together with some of the history of the times, and they became scripture. As each new prophet wrote, his records were added to the existing scripture. In this way there was a constantly growing volume of the sacred word. Eventually many of these writings were compiled into a book which we know as the Bible.

This process continued as long as the Lord had prophets on earth, both in Old and New Testament times. Never was it thought that this accumulated record contained all of the word of God, because, over the years, the Lord continued to send new prophets who received new revelations, which in turn became new and additional scripture. It was a set pattern of the Lord from the days of the patriarchs to the time of John the Revelator.

There are some who do not realize that there were prophets in the original Christian Church and that it was the intention of the Lord that they should continue in the Church until we all come to a unity of the faith.

But instead of unity among Christians, what do we have? We have division, which is overwhelming evidence of the need for the continued ministry of Christian prophets.

Do you remember how Paul explained this principle to the Ephesians? He said that the very foundation of the Church rested upon the apostles and prophets, with Jesus Christ as the chief cornerstone. (See Ephesians 2:20.)

Then, describing the organization of the Church, he said that the Savior "gave some apostles and some prophets and some evangelists and some pastors and teachers" as officers in the Church. He declared their purpose to be "for the perfecting of the saints, for the work of the ministry, for the edifying of the body" of the Church. (Ephesians 4:12.)

Is there ever a time when members can stop working toward perfection, when they no longer are benefited by activity in the Church, or when they do not require teaching and edifying?

Paul said that these officers who teach and edify are needed in the Church until we become perfect, until we reach the fulness of the measure of the stature of Christ. Heaven knows that none of us has achieved that distinction.

But what was another reason these officers should remain in the Church? Paul said they were given to us as a protection "that we henceforth be no more [as] children, tossed to and fro . . . with every wind of doctrine." (Ephesians 4:14.)

They will protect us from the false teachings of cultists and splinter groups and from the misleading philosophies of men.

The Church of Jesus Christ, then, should always be led by

living apostles and prophets who would receive the constant guidance of heaven. They would continue always in the Church as seers and revelators for the people.

But as they so ministered they would be providing also new and additional scripture appropriate to the times in which they lived, according to the Lord's pattern.

The prophets of the early Christian Church ministered in their day just as the Old Testament prophets did during the preceding centuries. And why? Because they followed this same divine pattern, for, as Amos explained, the Lord works only through prophets. (See Amos 3:7.)

When there are no prophets, there is no divine direction, and without such guidance the people walk in darkness.

It is an infallible sign of the true church that it has in it divinely chosen, living prophets to guide it, men who receive current revelation from God and whose recorded works become new scripture.

It is an infallible sign of the true church also that it will produce new and additional scripture arising out of the ministration of those prophets. This unfailing pattern of God is clearly made manifest through his dealings with his people from the beginning.

The Lord himself predicted that there would be other volumes of scripture in addition to the Bible. He knew, however, that some people would refuse to believe and would object to receiving more scripture. So he said:

"Many of the Gentiles shall say: A Bible! A Bible! We have got a Bible, and there cannot be any more Bible.

"Know ye not that there are more nations than one? Know ye not that I, the Lord your God, have created all men, and that I remember those who are upon the isles of the sea; and that I rule in the heavens above and in the earth beneath; and I bring forth my word unto the children of men, yea, even upon all the nations of the earth?

"Wherefore murmur ye, because that ye shall receive more of my word? Know ye not that the testimony of two nations is a witness unto you that I am God, that I remember one nation like unto another? Wherefore, I speak the same words unto one nation like unto another. And when the two nations shall run together the testimony of the two nations shall run together also.

"And I do this that I may prove unto many that I am the same yesterday, today, and forever; and that I speak forth my words according to mine own pleasure. And because that I have spoken one word ye need not suppose that I cannot speak another; for my work is not yet finished; neither shall it be until the end of man, neither from that time henceforth and forever.

"Wherefore, because that ye have a Bible ye need not suppose that it contains all my words; neither need ye suppose that I have not caused more to be written.

"For I commanded all men, both in the east and in the west, and in the north, and in the south, and in the islands of the sea, that they shall write the words which I speak unto them; for out of the books which shall be written I will judge the world, every man according to their works, according to that which is written.

"For behold, I shall speak unto the Jews and they shall write it; and I shall also speak unto the Nephites and they shall write it; and I shall also speak unto the other tribes of the house of Israel, which I have led away, and they shall write it; and I shall also speak unto all nations of the earth and they shall write it.

"And it shall come to pass that the Jews shall have the words of the Nephites, and the Nephites shall have the words of the Jews; and the Nephites and the Jews shall have the words of the lost tribes of Israel; and the lost tribes of Israel shall have the words of the Nephites and the Jews.

"And it shall come to pass that my people, which are of the house of Israel, shall be gathered home unto the lands of their possessions; and my word also shall be gathered in one. . . ." (2 Nephi 29:3, 8-14.)

So said the Lord.

We Latter-day Saints, of course, have the Bible as do other Christians. But we also have the writings of the Nephites, who were the ancient inhabitants of America, and who recorded their revelations and history in what today is known as the Book of Mormon. And what is the Book of Mormon?

The apostle Paul at one time defined faith as the evidence of things not seen. The Book of Mormon is solid, tangible evidence of both the seen and the unseen.

It is a book that can be felt and handled and read. It is a physical object, and so it cannot be explained out of existence. The critics cannot make it go away. As a published book it is here — tangible, physical, and material.

We can hold it in our hands. We can give it away as a gift. We can send it through the mail. If we wished we could drop it in the ocean or burn it in a fire, or we might even study it page by page for spiritual light and inspiration.

It is a physical volume that was printed on an electric press, in a commercial printing house, on paper made in a commercial paper mill, and with the use of ordinary printers' ink.

In other words, the Book of Mormon is a physical object, just as is the Bible or any other book. As a physical object, no one can say that it does not exist. Neither can it be explained away.

But where did it come from?

It was brought by an angel of God who came to earth for the particular purpose of delivering that book to Joseph Smith, the Mormon prophet.

But does anybody believe in angels in this enlightened age?

If you believe the Bible, you *must* believe in angels. And further, if you read the Bible you will know that it plainly says that an angel was designated to come to earth in the latter days to give a particular book to a particular man within a particular time frame.

To identify that man, the scripture refers to him as an unlearned man. Strange, isn't it, that the prophet Isaiah would do this? But that angel did come within the specified time. He came to Joseph Smith, who was the specified unlearned man. The book was then translated by Joseph Smith through the power of God and published to the world as the Book of Mormon.

Who was this angel of whom we speak? His name was Moroni. Inasmuch as he brought the Book of Mormon, his coming was tangible, physical, material evidence that there are angels of God and that one of them came to Joseph Smith and gave him this book.

And who was Moroni? He was one of the prophets who lived in ancient America, and died fifteen hundred years ago.

To appear in our day, then, obviously he had to come back from the dead. But our whole religion is based on angelic personages coming back from the dead. Then immortality is real, proved by the fact that an immortal personage delivered this tangible, material Book of Mormon to a modern, mortal man.

In coming back from the dead, Moroni was a physical being of literal, corporeal, material reality. He held those heavy gold plates in his hands. A block of metal measuring seven-by-seven-by-eight inches could weigh between thirty and fifty pounds. But Moroni held them in his hands and turned over the pages with his fingers. His were flesh and bone hands, resurrected hands.

The Book of Mormon, then, as a physical, material, tangible object, also becomes evidence of the resurrection of the dead.

Let us remember that twelve modern men saw and handled those same plates after Moroni had delivered them to Joseph Smith. In describing this experience, eight of them said that they handled them with their hands and added, "We have seen and hefted, and know of a surety that the said Smith has got the plates of which we have spoken." (Testimony of Eight Witnesses, Book of Mormon.)

They handled the plates with their hands. So did Moroni.

They turned over the pages, one by one. So did Moroni.

They examined the engravings on those plates, some of which were made by Moroni about fifteen hundred years ago.

So the published Book of Mormon is a physical witness to the fact of immortality, to the resurrection from the dead, and to the reality of God and his Son Jesus Christ.

In this day of doubt and criticism should we not be grateful for physical evidence of unseen things? Then should we not accept the Book of Mormon as such evidence?

The chief reason we have the Book of Mormon is that in the mouth of two or three witnesses shall all things be established. (See 2 Corinthians 13:1.) We have the Bible; we also have the Book of Mormon; and they constitute two voices — two volumes of scripture — from two widely separated ancient peoples, both bearing testimony to the divinity of the Lord Jesus Christ.

But we have two other scriptural witnesses also, making four altogether. They are the modern scriptures given as revelations through the Prophet Joseph Smith, and they, too, declare that Jesus is the Christ, the Savior, the Creator, the long-promised Messiah.

The world has been so confused by the conflicting creeds of men that the truth had to be given to mankind once again to disabuse their minds and correct their thinking. There was only one way in which this could be done and that was by new revelation. But to have new revelation requires the presence of a prophet to receive it, for, as Amos said, the Lord will not act except through prophets.

There was no prophet in all Christendom at the time the new revelation was to be given. So God raised up a new prophet to receive that revelation, to publish the Book of Mormon, and to direct the preaching of the true gospel in every nation.

And who was that prophet? Joseph Smith, Jr. He was the divinely called seer of latter days. He was the modern revelator. He was the translator and publisher of the Book of Mormon under the direction of Almighty God.

18

The Last Words
of Moroni

One of the most significant anniversaries recognized by our Church marks the visitations of the angel Moroni to the Prophet Joseph Smith preliminary to the restoration of the gospel of Jesus Christ in our day.

Moroni came back from the dead, a resurrected man!

He had lived in America some fifteen hundred years ago and was the sole survivor of his people in a series of tragic battles which took many lives.

He had witnessed the destruction of his whole nation, including his own family. In bitter vengeance their enemies had vowed their complete annihilation, and now this threat was accomplished.

Moroni's father was commander of the armies of this ancient people, known as Nephites. His name was Mormon. The war of which we speak took place here in America some four hundred years after Christ.

As the fighting neared its end, Mormon gathered the remnant of his forces about a hill which they called Cumorah, located in what is now the western part of the state of New York.

Their enemies, known as Lamanites, came against them on this hill. Of that dreadful event Mormon wrote:

"My people, with their wives and their children, did now behold the armies of the Lamanites marching towards them; and with that awful fear of death which fills the breasts of all the wicked, did they await to receive them.

" . . . Every soul was filled with terror because of the greatness of their numbers.

"And it came to pass that they did fall upon my people with the sword, and with the bow, and with the arrow, and with the ax, and with all manner of weapons of war.

"And it came to pass that my men were hewn down, yea, even my ten thousand who were with me, and I fell wounded in the midst. . . ." (Mormon 6:7-10.)

Then he spoke of other leaders serving with him in the Nephite army, all of whom had fallen with the forces under their command. He accounted for about a quarter of a million Nephite soldiers killed in that final encounter at Cumorah.

He mourned over this great loss and wrote:

"My soul was rent with anguish, because of the slain of my people, and I cried:

"O ye fair ones, how could ye have departed from the ways of the Lord! O ye fair ones, how could ye have rejected that Jesus, who stood with open arms to receive you!

"Behold, if ye had not done this, ye would not have fallen. But behold, ye are fallen, and I mourn your loss.

"O ye fair sons and daughters, ye fathers and mothers, ye husbands and wives, ye fair ones, how is it that ye could have fallen!

"But behold, ye are gone, and my sorrows cannot bring your return.

"O that ye had repented before this great destruction had come upon you. . . ." (Mormon 6:16-20, 22.)

Why were the Nephites destroyed?

They had been told that it is a privilege for anyone to live on the American continent, for it is a promised land, and those who reside here must abide by the rules that God decreed pertaining to it.

Only those who are willing to serve Jesus Christ, who is

the God of this land, may remain here. Others will be swept off.

The Nephites knew this, but with malice aforethought they reveled in sin and rejected the teachings of Christ.

Having failed to meet the conditions by which they could remain on this promised land, they were swept off, and with great violence.

At the time Mormon recorded the details of this dreadful tragedy he said that only twenty-four remained alive of all the men, women and children of the Nephites. These surviving few were themselves killed the next day — with one exception, Moroni, whom the Lord spared to close up the written record.

When finished with the record, Moroni was to hide it up in that same Hill Cumorah which was their battlefield. It would come forth in modern times as the Book of Mormon, named after Moroni's father, the historian who compiled it.

Realizing the importance of completing it, this lone survivor wrote: "I, Moroni, do finish the record of my father, Mormon." (Mormon 8:1.)

Then he wrote a description of the last battle and added, "I . . . remain alone to write the sad tale of the destruction of my people. . . . Therefore I will write and hide up the records in the earth. . . . My father hath been slain in battle, and all my kinsfolk, and I have not friends nor whither to go; and how long the Lord will suffer that I may live I know not." (Mormon 8:3-5.)

As he wrote his fateful words, he said again that his people were annihilated because they loved wickedness, rejected the counsel of God and gave themselves over to seeking wealth and corruption. This made up the deadly concoction which brought about their extinction.

Had not the Lord said to them, as he says to us now, that America is a choice land and that those who live here must obey God or be swept off? And had he not kept his word to those rebellious Nephites, now totally wiped out? So it is that today's archaeologists find the ruins which are silent witnesses to the greatness of these ancient people.

In closing his record, and knowing that it would come to us, Moroni pleaded with us, the modern inhabitants of this land, to escape the kind of tragic end which had obliterated his people. He said:

"Behold, I speak unto you as if ye were present, and yet ye are not. But behold, Jesus Christ hath shown you unto me, and I know your doing.

"And I know that ye do walk in the pride of your hearts. . . . Ye do love money, and your substance, and your fine apparel." (Mormon 8:35-37.)

In prophecy also he spoke of the tragic moral pollutions which would engulf many modern Americans. He asked why we are so foolish as to revel in sin, why we would reject the Christ, and thereby invite disaster.

"Why are ye ashamed to take upon you the name of Christ?" he asked, speaking to modern America, knowing full well that many might profess to believe in him and yet refuse to do his works. It is by engaging in his works that we truly take his name upon us. It is not through lip service. Moroni knew that faith without works is dead. And so likewise should we.

He made it clear that advance warning is given to us who live today, through the very book which he and his father had written and which he was about to bury in Cumorah. It would be published in our day to give us that warning.

Describing our day, he said the book would come forth when millions deny the power of God, when the world would be in turmoil, with earthquakes, violent storms, wars and rumors of wars in many places. (See Mormon 8:26-30.)

He said it would be in a time of great pollution. Isn't it interesting that he would speak of great pollution on the earth? Does it remind you of the claims of our modern ecologists?

He said also that it would be in a time of extensive crime, of murders, robberies, lies, deceptions, and immorality. Think of those words in terms of today's cover-ups, bribes, thievings, embezzlements, and other fraudulent practices among individuals, in business, and also in government. Hasn't dishonesty almost become a way of life with many people?

Think, too, of the epidemic of social diseases sweeping the nations in the wake of their vast immorality. What frightful pollutions these things are!

Before his death, Mormon wrote that his record would, of course, be a warning to those he called Gentiles, but that it would be a blessing to the Lamanites. Also he said that it would come with a special message to the Jews. For them it was published that they "may be persuaded that Jesus is the Christ, the Son of the living God; that the Father may bring about, through his most Beloved, his great and eternal purpose, in restoring the Jews, or all the house of Israel, to the land of their inheritance which the Lord their God hath given them, unto the fulfilling of his covenant." (Mormon 5:14.) Consider the current significance of that scripture!

Mormon then wrote directly to us as modern Americans who now occupy this promised land and said: "How can ye stand before the power of God, except ye shall repent and turn from your evil ways?

"Know ye not that ye are in the hands of God? Know ye not that he hath all power, and at his great command the earth shall be rolled together as a scroll?

"Therefore, repent ye, and humble yourselves before him, lest he shall come out in justice against you. . . ." (Mormon 5:22-24.)

Can we ignore such a warning, directed specifically at this generation?

Moroni joined his father with this:

"Who can stand against the works of the Lord? Who can deny his sayings? Who will rise up against the almighty power of the Lord? Who will despise the works of the Lord? Who will despise the children of Christ? Behold, all ye who are despisers of the works of the Lord, for ye shall . . . perish." (Mormon 9:26.)

It should be remembered that these men wrote to us out of the desperation of the event they were passing through as the Nephites were being wiped off the face of the earth. They knew that we would live here now under the same conditions that were given to them.

As Moroni wrote his last testimony, he realized how important his book is to our generation. He asked that we read it and believe it. So he pleaded:

"I would exhort you that ye would ask God, the Eternal Father, in the name of Christ, if these things are not true; and if ye shall ask with a sincere heart, with real intent, having faith in Christ, he will manifest the truth of it unto you, by the power of the Holy Ghost." (Moroni 10:4.) These were among his last words.

His pen had already inscribed this frightening but divine warning about America:

"This is a land which is choice above all other lands; wherefore he that doth possess it shall serve God or shall be swept off. . . ." (Ether 2:10.)

He gave us the lesson of the annihilation of the Nephites as a case in point. He wrote similarly of the tragedy of the Jaredites — another case in point. Do we realize that this same kind of destruction can come upon us, and for the same reason?

So this is the message of Moroni. He came back from the dead to deliver it — in these modern times. His people were Americans too. His words constituted a "people to people" message — ancient Americans speaking to modern Americans. Theirs was the voice of bitter experience seeking to persuade us to avoid the dreadful conditions which engulfed them.

Moroni announced that he will face us on judgment day in defense of his words. This he will do together with his book, for out of the books we shall be judged and the Book of Mormon is one of those books.

We now have it in our hands. It is published to the world. It carries God's message to all. It gives full and fair warning to this generation, and the warning is true!

Read it! Believe it! Pray over it! Obey its counsels! It can lead us unerringly to Christ.

The last words of Moroni. Dare we forget them? God grant that we never will.

19

Joseph's Ministry

The Lord Jesus Christ was appointed as our Savior in a premortal council in heaven.

The divine plan included two advents of the Lord into this world: One was his coming in mortality. The other will be his glorious second coming. For each there would be a forerunner to prepare the way in a sinful and apostate world. For his mortal advent that forerunner was John the Baptist. For his second coming, it was Joseph Smith.

The apostate people of John's day were divided into various contending factions. The Pharisees and the Sadducees were the two most prominent cults. But there were others.

John strongly resisted these apostates. He vigorously preached the coming of Christ and developed a following of believers in the Christ even before the Lord made his appearance. When the Savior subsequently came, John identified him to his own disciples by saying:

"Behold the Lamb of God, which taketh away the sin of the world. This is he of whom I said, After me cometh a man which is preferred before me." (John 1:29-30.)

This is he! The Lamb of God!

The converts made by John became the nucleus of the church which Jesus established in Palestine. That is how John prepared the way of the Lord.

The Second Coming was predicted by Jesus himself as is noted especially in Matthew, chapter 24.

A much greater advance preparation will be needed for his second coming than for the first. When Jesus came into mortality, his ministry was limited to the borders of Palestine, and John's work was limited in proportion.

But the Second Coming will be different. It will be seen worldwide.

"The sun [shall] be darkened, and the moon shall not give her light, and the stars shall fall from heaven, and the powers of the heavens shall be shaken:

"And then shall appear the sign of the Son of man in heaven: and then shall all the tribes of the earth mourn, and they shall see the Son of Man coming in the clouds of heaven with power and glory." (Matthew 24:29-30.)

Then an advance preparation on a worldwide basis is required as a prelude to such an appearance.

Malachi said, "Behold, I will send my messenger, *and he shall prepare the way before me:* and the Lord, whom ye seek, shall suddenly come to his temple. . . ." (Malachi 3:1; italics added.)

Then a great work of teaching and conversion must be done worldwide before the Lord's appearance in order to gather believers *in all nations* prepared to receive him.

And a temple — at least one — must be built as part of this preparation, for *to a temple the Lord will come.*

Who was this messenger appointed to prepare the way for the Lord's second coming?

Who was this temple builder?

Who was this prophet who would obtain the gospel by restoration and direct its preaching to all nations?

That messenger was Joseph Smith, Jr.

He was the preparer of the way for the Second Coming as definitely as John prepared the way for the first coming.

By restoration he received the everlasting gospel. By restoration he received divine authority.

He sent missionaries abroad in the world.

He was a temple builder, having directed the building of two himself and projected the erection of others.

Joseph Smith fits the pattern outlined by prophecy as the advance messenger for the Second Coming.

At this point, may I quote three contemporary statements giving the measure of this remarkable man as seen in his own day.

The first was written by Josiah Quincy in *Figures of the Past*. After visiting Joseph Smith in Nauvoo, he wrote:

"It is by no means improbable that some future textbook, for the use of generations yet unborn, will contain a question something like this: What historical American of the nineteenth century has exerted the most powerful influence upon the destinies of his countrymen? And it is by no means impossible that the answer to that interrogatory may be thus written: *Joseph Smith, the Mormon prophet*. And the reply, absurd as it doubtless seems to most men now living, may be an obvious commonplace to their descendants." (Josiah Quincy, *Figures of the Past* [Boston: Little, Brown, and Company, 1926], page 317.)

Second, *The New York Sun*, in September 1843, editorialized on Joseph Smith in this way:

"[He] must be set down as an extraordinary character, a prophet-hero, as Carlyle might call him. He is one of the great men of this age, and in future history will rank with those who, in one way or another, have stamped their impress strongly on society. . . .

"It is no small thing, in the blaze of the nineteenth century, to give to men a new revelation, found a new religion, establish new forms of worship, to build a city, with new laws, institutions and orders of architecture, — to establish ecclesiastic, civil and military jurisdiction, found colleges, send out missionaries, and make proselytes in two hemispheres: yet all this has been done by Joe Smith, and that against every sort of opposition, ridicule and persecution." (*DHC*, Vol. 6, page 3.)

Third, after his martyrdom, his close associates wrote the following:

"Joseph Smith, the Prophet and Seer of the Lord, has done more, save Jesus only, for the salvation of men in this world, than any other man that ever lived in it. In the short space of twenty years, he has brought forth the Book of Mormon, which he translated by the gift and power of God, and has been the means of publishing it on two continents; has sent the fulness of the everlasting gospel, which it contained, to the four quarters of the earth; has brought forth the revelations and commandments which compose this book of Doctrine and Covenants, and many other wise documents and instructions for the benefit of the children of men; gathered many thousands of the Latter-day Saints, founded a great city, and left a fame and name that cannot be slain. He lived great, and he died great in the eyes of God and his people; and like most of the Lord's anointed in ancient times, has sealed his mission and his works with his own blood; and so has his brother Hyrum. In life they were not divided, and in death they were not separated!" (D&C 135:3.)

That is the measure of Joseph Smith as seen by men who knew him best.

May I now call your attention to the words of the prophet Amos of the Old Testament:

"Surely the Lord God will do nothing, but he revealeth his secret unto his servants the prophets." (Amos 3:7.)

These few words give us a key to all the operations of God among human beings. He will do *nothing* — except through prophets. This was evident all through Old Testament times, for there he invariably worked through prophets.

This was equally true in New Testament times. Prophets were placed in the early Church as its foundation, but also for the perfection and edification of the Saints and to protect them from every wind of doctrine.

But following the establishment of the early Christian Church, in fact within its first century, a sweeping apostasy developed. Finally the original Christian Church disappeared. It was crowded out by man-made denominations with their uninspired creeds. The prophets disappeared.

However, a restoration of the gospel was predicted for the latter days, preceding the second coming of Christ. Peter had so declared. (See Acts 3:21.)

And how was the gospel to be brought back to earth?

By an angel, flying through the midst of heaven in the

hour of God's judgment, who would bring it back so that it might be preached abroad as a warning to all men before the coming of the Lord. (See Revelation 14:6-7.)

But to whom would the angel come?

Amos of Old Testament times said that the Lord would work only through prophets. But there were no prophets on earth when the time of restoration arrived, for Christianity had gone astray and no longer believed in prophets or current revelation. Then what could God do?

He must raise up a new prophet, and *that* he did in the person of Joseph Smith, Jr. When the restored Church was organized, the Lord said this to Joseph Smith:

"Behold, there shall be a record kept among you; and in it thou shalt be called a seer, a translator, a prophet, an apostle of Jesus Christ, an elder of the church through the will of God the Father, and the grace of your Lord Jesus Christ.

"Being inspired of the Holy Ghost to lay the foundation thereof, and to build it up unto the most holy faith." (D&C 21:1-2.)

So he was officially designated as prophet, seer and revelator in the Church by God himself.

Persecution was intense all through the ministry of the Prophet, but out of it came some of his most sublime moments.

The Prophet and some of his associates were confined to a jail at Richmond, Missouri, in 1838. Now I quote from *Essentials in Church History* by President Joseph Fielding Smith:

"The brethren were guarded by some of the vilest wretches that could be found, who spent their time in the presence of their prisoners relating their horrible deeds of wickedness. This thing continued for some time, when the Prophet, unable to stand it any longer, arose and rebuked them. The occurrence is graphically related by Elder Parley P. Pratt, in the following words:

" ' . . . On a sudden he [Joseph Smith] arose to his feet, and spoke in a voice of thunder, or as the roaring lion, uttering, as near as I can recollect, the following words:

" ' "SILENCE, ye fiends of the infernal pit. In the name of Jesus Christ I rebuke you, and command you to be still. I will not live another minute and hear such language. Cease such talk, or you or I die THIS INSTANT!"

" 'He ceased to speak. He stood erect in terrible majesty. Chained, and without a weapon; calm, unruffled and dignified as an angel, he looked upon the quailing guards; whose weapons were lowered or dropped to the ground, whose knees smote together, and who, shrinking into a corner, or crouching at his feet, begged his pardon, and remained quiet till a change of guards.

" 'I have seen the ministers of justice, clothed in magisterial robes, and criminals arraigned before them, while life was suspended on a breath, in the courts of England; I have witnessed a Congress in solemn session to give laws to nations; I have tried to conceive of kings, of royal courts, of thrones and crowns; and of emperors assembled to decide the fate of kingdoms; but dignity and majesty have I seen but once, as it stood in chains, at midnight, in a dungeon in an obscure village of Missouri.' " (Smith, *Essentials*, pages 203-4.)

One of the high points in the spiritual experience of the Prophet came while he was incarcerated in Liberty Jail. Out of it came two of the most glorious of all his revelations, for the Lord spoke comfort to him in the midst of his afflictions.

At first the Prophet cried out for help:

"O God, where art thou? And where is the pavilion that covereth thy hiding place?

"How long shall thy hand be stayed, and thine eye, yea thy pure eye, behold from the eternal heavens the wrongs of thy people and of thy servants, and thine ear be penetrated with their cries?

"Yea, O Lord, how long shall they suffer these wrongs and unlawful oppressions, before thine heart shall be softened toward them, and thy bowels be moved with compassion toward them?

"Remember thy suffering saints, O our God; and thy servants will rejoice in thy name forever."

And then the Lord spoke:

"My son, peace be unto thy soul; thine adversity and thine afflictions shall be but a small moment;

"And then, if thou endure it well, God shall exalt thee on high; thou shalt triumph over all thy foes.

"Thy friends do stand by thee, and they shall hail thee again with warm hearts and friendly hands.

"Thou art not yet as Job; thy friends do not contend against thee, neither charge thee with transgression, as they did Job." (D&C 121:1-3, 6-10.)

Then we have this marvelous language from the Lord:

"The ends of the earth shall inquire after thy name, and fools shall have thee in derision, and hell shall rage against thee;

"While the pure in heart, and the wise, and the noble, and the virtuous, shall seek counsel, and authority, and blessings constantly from under thy hand.

"And thy people shall never be turned against thee by the testimony of traitors .... and thy God shall stand by thee forever and ever." (D&C 122:1-4.)

Again we have this from the Lord to his suffering Prophet:

"How long can rolling waters remain impure? What power shall stay the heavens? As well might man stretch forth his puny arm to stop the Missouri river in its decreed course, or to turn it up stream, as to hinder the Almighty from pouring down knowledge from heaven upon the heads of the Latter-day Saints.

"Behold, there are many called, but few are chosen. And why are they not chosen?

"Because their hearts are set so much upon the things of this world, and aspire to the honors of men, that they do not learn this one lesson —

"That the rights of the priesthood are inseparably connected with the powers of heaven, and that the powers of heaven cannot be controlled nor handled only upon the principles of righteousness." (D&C 121:33-36.)

Not even Shakespeare could write like that!

Joseph Smith's visions of the three degrees of glory lifted gospel understanding to a new high. What is known as section 88 of the Doctrine and Covenants also is one of the most impressive declarations of doctrine we have.

The Prophet's visions of the Savior, of course, rank as his most important revelations. Note what he says in section 76 as he and Sidney Rigdon were together. This vision came in the Johnson home near Kirtland, Ohio.

"And now, after the many testimonies which have been given of him, this is the testimony, last of all, which we give of him: That he lives!

"For we saw him, even on the right hand of God; and we heard the voice bearing record that he is the Only Begotten of the Father —

"That by him, and through him, and of him, the worlds are and were created, and the inhabitants thereof are begotten sons and daughters unto God." (D&C 76:22-24.)

And then from section 110, given in the Kirtland Temple, we have:

"We saw the Lord standing upon the breastwork of the pulpit, before us; and under his feet was a paved work of pure gold, in color like amber.

"His eyes were as a flame of fire; the hair of his head was white like the pure snow; his countenance shone above the brightness of the sun; and his voice was as the sound of the rushing of great waters, even the voice of Jehovah, saying:

"I am the first and the last; I am he who liveth, I am he who was slain; I am your advocate with the Father." (D&C 110:2-4.)

Visitations by Moses and Elijah of old were experienced also, as well as those by "divers other angels," each one committing the keys of his dispensation. So this became a consolidation of all previous dispensations. That is why it is called the dispensation of the fulness of times.

Joseph's vision of the celestial kingdom is most notable.

" 'I beheld the celestial kingdom of God, and the glory thereof, whether in the body or out I cannot tell. I saw the transcendent beauty of the gate through which the heirs of that kingdom will enter, which was like unto circling flames of fire; also the blazing throne of God, whereon was seated the Father and the Son. I saw the beautiful streets of that kingdom, which had the appearance of being paved with gold. I saw Fathers Adam and Abraham, and my father and mother, my brother, Alvin, that has long since slept, and marveled how it was that he had obtained an inheritance in the kingdom, seeing that he had departed this life before the Lord had set his hand to gather Israel the second time and had not been baptized for the remission of sins.

" 'Thus came the voice of the Lord to me, saying —

" ' "All who have died without a knowledge of this Gospel, who would have received it if they had been permitted to tarry, shall be heirs of the celestial kingdom of God; also all that shall die henceforth without a knowledge of it, who would have received it with all their hearts, shall be heirs of that kingdom; for I, the Lord, will judge all men according to their works; according to the desire of their hearts."

" 'And I also beheld that all children who die before they arrive at the years of accountability are saved in the celestial kingdom of heaven.' " (Smith, *Essentials*, page 158.)

When the Saints left Missouri and moved to Illinois, they established a city which they called Nauvoo. Its original name was Commerce. When the Saints first arrived there, many fell ill because of the swampy conditions.

We quote from *Essentials in Church History:*

"The Saints began to immigrate to Nauvoo, and the city grew rapidly by such additions. About one year after the location of the site, Nauvoo had a population of over three thousand souls, and six years later, at the time of the great western exodus, about twenty thousand. . . .

"Due to the unhealthful condition of the place when the people first arrived at Commerce, many were taken sick with malaria fever, and were nigh unto death. Some of the refugees were sheltered only by tents and wagon covers, for there had been little time, and less means, by which houses, even of logs, could be built. On the morning of July 22, 1839, the Prophet arose from his own bed of sickness and being filled with the Spirit of the Lord, he went forth along the river bank healing all who were afflicted. Among the number were Henry G. Sherwood and Benjamin Brown, who appeared in a dying condition. He later crossed over the river to Montrose and healed Brigham Young and a number of other brethren of the twelve, and took them along with him to assist him in this ministry. What took place in Iowa is thus related by Elder Wilford Woodruff:

" 'After healing all the sick upon the bank of the river as far as the stone house, he called upon Elder Kimball and some others to accompany him across the river to visit the sick at Montrose. Many of the Saints were living at the old military barracks. Among the number were several of the twelve. On his arrival, the first house he visited was that occupied by Elder Brigham Young, the president of the quorum of the twelve, who lay sick. Joseph healed him, then he arose and accompanied the Prophet on his visit to others who were in the same condition. They visited Elder W. Woodruff, also Elders Orson Pratt and John Taylor, all of whom were living in Montrose. They also accompanied him. The next place they visited was the home of Elijah Fordham, who was supposed to be about breathing his last. When the company entered the room the Prophet of God walked up to the dying man, and took hold of his right hand and spoke to him; but Brother Fordham was unable to speak, his eyes were set in his head like glass, and he seemed entirely unconscious of all around him. Joseph held his hand and looked into his eyes in silence for a length of time. A change in the countenance of Brother Fordham was soon perceptible to all present. His sight returned, and upon Joseph asking him if he knew him, he, in a low whisper, answered, "Yes." Joseph asked him if he had faith to be healed. He answered, "I fear it is too late; if you had come sooner I think I would have been healed." The Prophet said, "Do you believe in Jesus Christ?" He answered in a feeble voice, "I do." Joseph then stood erect, still holding his hand in silence several moments; then he spoke in a very loud voice, saying: "Brother Fordham, I command you in the name of Jesus Christ to arise from this bed and be made whole." . . . Brother Fordham arose from his bed and was immediately made whole. His feet were bound in poultices, which he kicked off, then putting on his clothes, he ate a bowl of bread and milk, and followed the Prophet into the street.'

"In this manner the Prophet and the brethren passed from house to house, healing the sick and recalling them from the mouth of the tomb. It was on this occasion that a man, not a member of the Church, seeing the mighty miracles which were performed, begged the Prophet to go with him and heal two of his children who were very sick. The Prophet could not go, but said he would send some one to heal them. Taking from his pocket a silk handkerchief he handed it to Elder

Wilford Woodruff and requested him to go and heal the children. He told Elder Woodruff to wipe the faces of the children with the handkerchief, and they should be healed. This he did and they were healed. . . .

"Nauvoo was incorporated in December, 1840. On the 16th day of that month Governor Thomas Carlin signed the bill. Stephen A. Douglas was secretary of state; and Abraham Lincoln, a member of the legislature, had favored the bill. . . . [The city became the largest in Illinois.]

"The city council was authorized to establish and organize the 'University of the City of Nauvoo,' for 'the teaching of the arts, sciences and learned professions.' . . . [Elementary schools were quickly organized.]

"Another provision granted the city council the power to 'organize . . . a body of . . . men, to be called the "Nauvoo Legion." ' . . . Joseph Smith was elected lieutenant general." (Smith, *Essentials*, pages 223-25.)

One of the first ordinances introduced in the city council of Nauvoo provided protection for people of all religious faiths, showing the attitude of the Saints toward other churches regardless of the fact that much of the persecution from which they suffered was generated by gentlemen of the cloth.

Nauvoo was a most interesting and progressive city. It had a population of twenty thousand with more than two thousand well-built houses, and only a few log cabins. Most of the homes were of brick construction, and reflected the high culture of the Saints.

You will be interested to know that it had:

1 university	6 silversmiths
20 schools	1 watch and clock maker
1 circulating library	3 glass factories
35 general stores	3 hotels
9 dressmaking and millinery shops	3 halls for opera and drama
	8 tailor shops
3 newspapers	9 law offices
13 physicians	4 bakeries
5 potteries	11 grist mills
4 stationers	6 blacksmith shops
7 wagon and carriage shops	2 iron mongers
	3 coopers

5 livery stables and saddle shops	3 furniture factories
	1 goldsmith
4 lime kilns	1 comb factory
3 soap and candle factories	1 straw packer
7 brick yards	5 midwives
3 lumber yards	3 notary publics

Although many brethren had been called to missionary service earlier, the Prophet now began the worldwide preaching of the gospel and sent elders beyond the United States to Canada, Europe, South America and the South Seas. He declared that the gospel must be taken to every clime, to every nation, kindred, tongue and people, and this was his way of beginning that very great undertaking.

Also at the general conference of the Church held in Nauvoo, April 6-8, 1840, Elder Orson Hyde was appointed to dedicate Palestine for the gathering of the Jews.

Persecution continued unabated, however, and the Saints were constantly harassed by their enemies. The Prophet looked to the federal government for help.

He was devoted to the Constitution of the United States and under its provisions hoped to receive protection. He had declared it to be an inspired document, a glorious banner.

Since the law did not adequately protect the Saints in Missouri, the Prophet issued an appeal to the people of the entire United States, asking them for fair treatment under the Constitution, and to stop the merciless persecution. Said he:

"I ask the citizens of this Republic whether such a state of things is to be suffered to pass unnoticed, and the hearts of widows, orphans, and patriots to be broken, and their wrongs left without redress? No! I invoke the genius of our Constitution. I appeal to the patriotism of Americans to stop this unlawful and unholy procedure; and pray that God may defend this nation from the dreadful effects of such outrages." (*DHC*, Vol. 3, page 332.)

He made a trip to Washington, D.C., and waited upon President Martin Van Buren in behalf of the Saints. He portrayed their sufferings at the hands of mobs, and asked for federal redress and protection inasmuch as the state provided none.

The Prophet said of this meeting:

"I had an interview with Martin Van Buren, the President, who treated me very insolently, and it was with great reluctance he listened to our message, which, when he had heard, he said: 'Gentlemen, your cause is just, but I can do nothing for you;' and 'If I take up for you I shall lose the vote of Missouri.' His whole course went to show that he was an office-seeker, that self-aggrandizement was his ruling passion, and that justice and righteousness were no part of his composition." (*DHC*, Vol. 4, page 80.)

The Saints also made an earnest appeal to Congress but it likewise came to naught.

Finally, as a last effort to call the attention of the nation to the sad plight of the Latter-day Saints, the Prophet declared himself a candidate for the presidency of the United States.

He apparently had no expectation of winning that position, but his desire was to dramatize the persecutions of the Saints before the whole nation in the hope of raising public sentiment in their favor.

He was nominated for president by his own people in a convention held in Nauvoo on January 29, 1844, and then by an Illinois state convention on May 17, 1844.

What were Joseph Smith's political views?

He advocated reduction in the number of congressmen by two-thirds.

He urged laws to provide for useful employment of state prisoners on roads and other public works rather than to have prisoners languish in jail.

He urged the death penalty for murder.

He urged that prisons be turned into seminaries of learning.

He urged all slave-holding states to free the slaves by 1850, with the U.S. government compensating slave owners by revenue to be obtained through the sale of public lands.

He urged that all men render good for evil, and that honor should become their standard.

He urged less federal spending and lower taxes.

He urged the establishment of a national bank, with branches in all states and territories.

He urged the use of federal troops to put down mobocracy, rebellion, or invasion.

He urged that Oregon be admitted to the Union, and that steps be taken to include Texas, Canada and Mexico as part of the United States.

On this platform he began his campaign for the presidency, but martyrdom a few weeks later ended his career.

Joseph's great early contribution, of course, was the Book of Mormon.

In bringing forth that volume under the direction of the Lord, Joseph fulfilled literally and completely the prophecy of Isaiah, chapter 29. He met the prediction of Ezekiel likewise, and today the Book of Mormon stands as scripture equal in importance to the Bible. Because of the many uninspired translations of the Bible, the Book of Mormon stands out, as the Prophet himself said, as the most correct book on earth.

It is a literal translation from ancient gold plates given him by the angel Moroni. It is the word of God. It was written by the command of Jesus Christ himself. (2 Nephi 29:10-14.) Now it comes to all mankind as a material witness for the divinity of the Savior, and as physical evidence of the veracity of Joseph Smith.

Not only do we have the testimony of the Prophet and the eleven witnesses concerning the truth of that book, but we have the word of his mother and wife.

Lucy Mack Smith, his mother, declared:

"That book ... [the Book of Mormon] was brought forth by the power of God, and translated by the gift of the Holy Ghost; and, if I could make my voice sound as loud as the trumpet of Michael the Archangel, I would declare the truth from land to land, and from sea to sea." (Smith, *History of Joseph Smith*, page 204.)

As we have already indicated, his wife, Emma, said:

"My belief is that the Book of Mormon is of divine authenticity — I have not the slightest doubt of it. I am satisfied that no man could have dictated the writing of the manuscripts unless he was inspired; for, when acting as his scribe, ... [Joseph] would dictate to me hour after hour; and when returning after meals, or interruptions, he would at once begin where he had left off, without either seeing the manuscript or having any portion of it read to him. . . . It would have been improbable that a learned man could do this, and for one so . . . unlearned as he was, it was simply impossible." (Preston Nibley, *The Witnesses of the Book of Mormon* [Salt Lake City: Deseret Book Company, 1973], page 29.)

The Prophet had repeated impressions from the Spirit that he would be martyred. One of those times was when he predicted that the Saints would move to the Rocky Mountains and there become a great people. He, therefore, took the necessary precautions so far as the future development of the Church was concerned.

He held all the keys and powers which the angels had bestowed upon him. Those keys were not only for the establishment of the work, but for its continued advancement as well. The work would be thwarted if he died without leaving those powers to those who would survive him.

Therefore, he called the Twelve together and made it known that *they* were chosen to carry on the ministry after his death. To give them the necessary authority to do so, he laid his hands upon each of them and conferred upon them every key, power, and priesthood which he had received from the angels, thus making the Twelve legal successors in the work, and empowering them to expand the kingdom.

Persecution continued until finally he and his brother Hyrum were martyred in Carthage Jail.

But he had done his work. He had prepared the way for the coming of the Lord.

And at time of writing, the membership of the Church which began with only six persons numbers four million and is doubling every twelve years. The missionaries we have in the field number twenty-seven thousand. We are in sixty nations.

But the work is also spread by radio, television, leased telephone wires, and the printed word, so that people in all the free world are given access to the gospel.

Temple building, which Joseph began, has continued until we now have either in operation or in prospect, temples in the United States, Canada, England, New Zealand, Switzerland,

Mexico, Japan, Brazil, and Samoa. Without doubt, more will be added as the need requires.

With all this preparation, the Prophet's work has been well done. The cause he served is still going forward and will yet reach even greater heights.

Hail to the man who communed with Jehovah! He was the chosen forerunner of the Lord, the modern counterpart of John the Baptist. He was a great and faithful servant, a mighty seer and revelator of Almighty God, the head of this dispensation — Joseph Smith, Jr.

His people, now numbering in the millions, worldwide, will be ready to greet the Lord when he comes, and *come he will!*

"But who may abide the day of his coming? and who shall stand when he appeareth? for he is like a refiner's fire, and like fullers' soap:

"And he shall sit as a refiner and purifier of silver: and he shall purify the sons of Levi, and purge them as gold and silver, that they may offer unto the Lord an offering in righteousness." (Malachi 3:2-3.)

The Lord will come, and Joseph has prepared the way for him.

Epilogue

MORONI'S FAREWELL

"I would exhort you that ye would come unto Christ, and lay hold upon every good gift, and touch not the evil gift, nor the unclean thing.

"And awake, and arise from the dust, O Jerusalem; yea, and put on thy beautiful garments, O daughter of Zion; and strengthen thy stakes and enlarge thy borders forever, that thou mayest no more be confounded, that the covenants of the Eternal Father which he hath made unto thee, O house of Israel, may be fulfilled.

"Yea, come unto Christ, and be perfected in him, and deny yourselves of all ungodliness; and if ye shall deny yourselves of all ungodliness, and love God with all your might, mind and strength, then is his grace sufficient for you, that by his grace ye may be perfect in Christ; and if by the grace of God ye are perfect in Christ, ye can in no wise deny the power of God.

"And again, if ye by the grace of God are perfect in Christ, and deny not his power, then are ye sanctified in Christ by the grace of God, through the shedding of the blood of Christ, which is in the covenant of the Father unto the remission of your sins, that ye become holy, without spot.

"And now I bid unto all, farewell. I soon go to rest in the paradise of God, until my spirit and body shall again reunite, and I am brought forth triumphant through the air, to meet you before the pleasing bar of the great Jehovah, the Eternal Judge of both quick and dead. Amen."

Index